crazy

"I remember when . . . I remember, I remember when I lost my mind . . . "

I was flipping channels on my car radio when I heard a song playing. There was something about the singer's voice and my mood that made me feel like I was in a lucid dream.

An ordinary morning would find me listening to National Public Radio, catching up on world events, and mentally preparing myself for my daily activities. I don't listen to pop music, but this particular day I could definitely identify with the loss of my mind.

"Maybe I'm crazy . . . "

I started to laugh when he got to that part. My mouth unconsciously opened and a sound that resembled a wild banshee's cry escaped my lips. The sound was loud and uncontrollable, as if it had been buried deep inside my psyche and finally found its way to the surface.

You think you're crazy? Haha . . . Boy, if you only knew!

I could not remember who told me, but someone said that talking to myself does not necessarily make me crazy. Technically, I would only become crazy when I start to answer myself. I didn't want to be crazy, but I thought that for once it would be nice to get outside of myself instead of always doing what was expected of me. People live recklessly all the time. Why should I have to be different?

Morning traffic in the city was always hectic and rushed, but that day I felt no particular need to hurry. Suddenly, traffic slowed to a crawl and I noticed that there was an accident ahead. I looked to my right and noticed drivers banging on their steering wheels and glancing back and forth between their clocks and the road. I pushed my Satellite XM Radio to a smooth jazz station to relax myself. I figured that I would be in traffic for some time, so I loosened my seat belt and settled in my seat.

As I looked to my left, I noticed a mother driving with two young girls in the backseat. The car first grabbed my attention because of its color . . . it was a bright yellow Volkswagen Beetle. The rims of the car were the same bright yellow hue, and I was reminded of sunshine as grey storm clouds gathered above me.

The younger of the two girls fixed her blue eyes on me, and made a motion to wipe her blond hair from her eyes. She looked so young and innocent, and held what looked to be a grey elephant in her hands. I instantly felt a connection with her, knowing what it felt like to need something to hold on to for security.

As her eyes met mine, she raised her hand to wave at me and the gesture made my eyes well with water. She did not smile while she was waving . . . she just stared at me, as if she was merely letting me know that I existed.

I kept my left hand on the steering wheel as I raised my right hand and waved back at her. The little girl instantly smiled a satisfied smile, as if her whole purpose for the morning was to acknowledge me in traffic. For a brief moment, I felt peaceful. Almost as if my world was not the disaster that I imagined.

As if on cue, traffic started to move along as normal. The mother drove the yellow Beetle into oblivion, and as the car moved away I noticed something on the shoulder of the road ahead of me. As I got closer, I noticed random articles of men's clothing next to the median. First a pair of blue and red gym shorts . . . then what looked to be a work boot of some kind. A little further up the road there was a pillow, and then the other boot appeared.

I bet his wife caught him cheating and threw his stuff out on the road. I let out a soft laugh to myself.

Serves him right! What made him think he could cheat and get away with it?

The "Crazy" song came back to my mind. I felt crazy. Here I was, driving down a busy highway having a conversation with myself about a hypothetical situation. How quickly my mind jumped to the worst case scenario, automatically assuming that a cheating man was the reason for the clothes on the side of the road.

I realized that was what I would have done if I had the nerve . . . what I SHOULD have done. I saw my exit, and eased right toward the city street. As I merged into the left lane, the strangest thought came to my mind:

No, I should have thrown HIM out into oncoming traffic.

My mind started to wander as the grey asphalt with its yellow lines intermingled until there was no distinction between the two of them. The colors and separating indications did not matter. I became unconcerned with what side of the road I was on, as long as I was driving. I became mesmerized by the road, almost falling into a dreamlike state when I heard a loud horn, and I jumped.

I saw the truck coming full speed toward me, the big box frame barreling in my direction. For a moment, everything was a white blur until it got close. I immediately jerked the steering wheel right, narrowly missing a collision. The truck driver screamed something inaudible at me and I raised my hand as if to say, "I'm sorry".

But I really wasn't.

That particular day, I woke up with a feeling like I wanted to die. I would never actually put a gun to my head or hang myself, but it would be nice to never have to feel. I would love to go a whole twenty-four hours without feeling sad or unloved or guilty or inadequate.

I looked up and saw a McDonald's sign in front of me, and decided to pull into its parking lot. The yellow arches were talking to me . . . quite loudly.

Girl . . . a Big Mac and a large fry would taste so good to you right now! Just imagine those perfect fries . . . so crispy and salty. Not to mention that special sauce in between those soft buns and patties.

I felt my stomach respond with a feeling of excitement . . . the same excitement that I felt when I thought about eating something numbing. I looked at the clock on the dashboard and realized that it was only 8:45 a.m.

I took a second glance at my beautiful, leather dashboard. It was all shiny and 'Armor All'ed" up, and my cream colored carpet was clean and dirt free. My custom made Lexus IS C, red and sleek, was a crowning achievement for me. It was not the most expensive car that Lexus made, but it was the first car that I had purchased for myself.

When people looked at it, I felt like I was someone important. But strangely, it was starting to feel like more of a haven than just a vehicle. It was one of the few things that I had that I could call mine, and the thought saddened me. It was just a possession. It could not hold me at night nor tell me that it loved me.

I sank down into the seat, wanting to melt and blend into the surroundings. I wished that I was just a regular person that day . . . without the pressures or responsibilities of maintaining an 'image'. I wished that I could just be worry-free and happy for once.

I looked out of my front windshield and I saw a young girl pushing a baby in one of those folding strollers . . . the ones that look about the size of an umbrella.

From my line of vision the girl walked briskly through the parking lot as if in a hurry. On her face was a look of panic, and for no apparent reason, she broke into a frantic dash. I sat up straight and watched her run at full speed, her gazelle-like stride carrying her across the black pavement.

As I glanced to my right, I saw her reason for hurry. The city bus went by at lightening speed, and the girl stopped suddenly, unable to catch its descent.

As if on cue, the skies opened and softly sprinkled a mist over my windshield. I watched the girl, walking dejectedly in the direction she came from. Her shoulders were slumped and it was hard to tell whether she had rain or tears on her face.

Without a second thought, I started my car and drove to where she was. The events of the night before had given me a boldness that I had not previously possessed. The 'sane' me would have probably said a quick prayer for the girl and kept driving. I had wished this morning to be a little more reckless, and this was my chance.

"Do you need a ride somewhere?"

I yelled out of my opened window and waited for her to respond. I saw her eyes scan over me and my car, and then look around to survey the surroundings. She looked deflated, but was hesitant about accepting my offer.

She was not dirty, but I could tell by the quality of her clothes that she was not someone that I would normally associate with. She was wearing jeans that were too short for her long legs, so she rolled the bottoms up. Her shoes appeared to be used, and worn from excessive walking. She had on a t-shirt with faded letters, but her clothes seemed to be the best that she could find.

Since being married and living the 'good life', I purposed to avoid anything that reminded me of poverty. But as I was determined to die that day, I figured I would do a good deed before I ended it all.

"Sweetheart", I yelled, "it's raining out here and your baby is getting wet. I can give you a ride to wherever you want to go . . . no strings attached."

Her shoulders suggested defeat, but her eyes screamed distrust. I remembered being young and proud once. I had to appeal to her sense of reason.

"Young Lady, please look at me. I won't fight you to take a ride. But if you don't do it for yourself, at least do it for your baby."

She walked slowly to my car, all the while looking around as if she was expecting something crazy to occur. As she reached the passenger side, she was hesitant to get in. I pushed the automatic unlock function and told her that she could sit comfortably in the backseat with her child, since we did not have a car seat.

As she settled into the car, I asked her where she was going. She informed me that she was trying to get to an appointment with Social Services. She opened her mouth to tell me more, but hesitated as if she did not want to divulge too much information. A part of me did not want to know, either. I figured that I would just take this girl where she needed to go, and move on.

The ride was quiet. I flipped through some stations, just to make sound in the car. I started to question why I had even stopped to pick her up. I decided to make small talk so that I did not have to listen to the madness in my own head.

"So do you live on that side of town where I picked you up?"

She paused for a while before she answered. I started to get a little worried, wondering if I had just picked up a fugitive from the law.

"Well, Ma'am, me and my son Jesse just started staying at the shelter over there a few days ago." She paused, and then her words started to spill out in an apologetic way. "I must have messed up on the bus schedule . . . I don't really know my way around this part of town and . . ."

All of the sudden, the girl in my backseat broke out in tears. I didn't even try to stop her, because I felt like crying myself. In my quest to forget poverty I forgot what life used to be like. It was not that long ago that I had to catch a bus or use food stamps. Although it had been many years ago, those type of memories don't easily leave your mind.

I was starting to get uncomfortable with the memories, so I decided to change the subject.

"So, Jesse is your son's name? My father's name is also Jesse. I'll tell you what, you should dry your tears because you have a beautiful son. And as long as you have him, you should never lose focus."

As I glanced in my rearview mirror, I saw her eyes brighten and turn toward Jesse. There was something about a mother's love . . . how no matter what she faced, she could always count on the child whom she bore. As soon as a smile touched her lips, it faded and the seriousness of the situation rested on her face.

I noticed how she glanced around my car and settled her eyes on me. My hair was straight and long, my fingernails perfectly manicured. My custom made suit still smelled of the dry cleaners and my jewelry sparkled in the light. I wondered if she felt out of place.

She sat back and looked out of the window, and I focused my eyes straight ahead. I drove with mixed emotions . . . feeling as if God was asking me to choose my path for the day. I had a choice, to end my life or to help someone begin theirs.

After wrestling with myself, I glanced back at the girl in my backseat and decided to call my office. I picked up my cell phone and spoke into it, saying, "Call the office." As the phone rang, my heart raced. I had never called in to work without there being a serious illness or unexpected meeting. I heard my assistant answer the phone.

"Claudia Brixton's office, this is Julie. How may I direct your call?"

"Julie, this is Claudia. How are you doing today?" I saw my passenger's ears prick up, and I saw her shoulders relax as she realized that I was not a crazy serial killer . . .

I was a real person with a real job that would not hurt her.

As I spoke to Julie, she informed me of her status and commenced to give me my schedule for the day. I listened with half-interest, knowing that my day had been divinely planned for me already.

"Julie, I need you to cancel my appointments and reschedule my meetings for today. Something very important came up that I need to attend to." With that, I turned and smiled at my backseat passenger, and then directed my attention back to my phone call.

"Please forward my calls to voicemail and I will check back in with you this afternoon."

My mind eased and my spirit brightened as I figured out what I was going to do that day. In church we always talked about 'do unto others' . . . Well, today I would do . . . and do it well.

"If you did not hear already, my name is Claudia. What is your name?" I tried to speak in the kindest voice that I could imagine. I decided that day that I would make it all about someone else, instead of focusing on what was going on in my life. I would just cross that "Crazy" bridge when I got to it.

After the wall of defense had been broken down, she told me that her name was Paris. She did not look to be what I would assume a 'Paris' would look like. That name was a name that I would associate with wealth and fame, but I learned not to put too much weight on assumptions.

Paris was tall and slim, and approximately the color of a Hershey's Kiss. Her hair was arranged in a ponytail of discolored, outgrown hair extensions. She tried to pull them back as neatly as possible, but it was apparent that she needed some attending to.

"Well, Paris, if you would allow me to, I would like to help you today. I do not expect anything in return, except that by the end of the day, you feel as beautiful and worthy as you are. Please allow me to do something kind for you."

My last statement sounded like a desperate plea, but I was feeling very low and desperate. I felt the need to mean something to someone, even if it was only temporary. As Paris consented, I smiled on the inside. All of the hurt and pain that I felt, I would turn it into joy for someone else.

Our first stop was to pick up a car seat. Even in my quest for death, I could not risk their lives. As we walked through

Babies-R-Us, I felt that familiar sadness. It was a store that I would never frequent, unless I was buying something for someone else. I felt myself slipping into that melancholy state, and I had to pull myself back to reality.

I smiled at Paris and helped her pick out a car-seat and some things for Jesse. Paris seemed genuinely ecstatic, thankful that she could give Jesse the things she desired to give him but could not afford. When thinking about how much money I've wasted on shoes and jewelry, the things that she asked for paled in comparison.

After Jesse was secure in his car seat, I drove both of them to The Onyx, an upscale restaurant located in the Downtown area. I wanted Paris to get a taste of the 'high life', and see the places she could access one day.

As we walked into the restaurant, it felt as if all eyes were on us. The Onyx was a place that I frequented with Terry, whenever he was feeling guilty about something. So needless to say, we ate there often. I won't lie . . . being there with Paris was awkward. The patrons looked at her as if she was a charity case.

I was somewhat self-conscious to be associated with someone so out of my social class. I had second thoughts about what people would say, not wanting them to think that we were cut from the same cloth, so-to-speak.

The instant that those thoughts came to mind, I looked at Paris and watched as her eyes scanned the room. She held Jesse closer to her to shield him from the eyes of the others in the restaurant. When her eyes shifted down to the floor, an unfamiliar righteous indignation rose up in me.

"Paris, don't you EVER look down. You keep your head up at all times. Never be ashamed." I held her hand and led her to the head waiter who recognized me.

"Mrs. Brixton, good day! Would you like a table near the window or the front?" I could feel Paris straighten up and stand closer to me, so that she did not feel out of place.

"Jonathan, bless you. I would love a table by the window so that we can see the view of the garden terrace. I also need a chair for the young gentleman and a menu for the lady. I will have my usual."

I heard the sound before I recognized where it came from. "I'll have what she havin'. I don't need no menu." Paris spoke in a soft, but confident voice. I smiled inwardly, thinking to myself that I had made a difference.

My mind drifted back to when I was first introduced to 'The Life', as Terry called it. Everything in that world is based on your appearance, and it can be very intimidating.

As we sat, I watched her face fill with awe as she took in the beauty of the restaurant. "This must be how it feel to be rich," she said as she noticed the well-dressed people. "Everybody here look super rich. I don't know if I shoulda came here."

I remembered how it felt to be young and insecure . . . coming from the wrong side of the tracks. Feeling that if the world knew where you really came from, they would no longer let you in their circle. I decided to stop caring what people thought.

"Paris, I am going to tell you something that not too many people know about me. I did not grow up with privilege. When I came into this circle, I was the girl from the ghetto that people laughed about and turned their noses up at." She looked at my polished appearance and shook her head as if to say that I was lying.

"Yes, Paris . . . Fortunately, I had people along my path who took the time to show me how to 'look' like a lady and 'talk' like a lady. I was not born with a silver spoon in my mouth like some of them. But guess what? You can even surpass some of these bourgeois people who look at you like you are supposed to take out their trash. Poverty is all in the mind. You have to believe you can be more than what you are, because that's exactly what I did."

I was amazed at the words that came out of my mouth. Most of my closest friends in 'The Life' had no knowledge of my past, nor had they met my family. Everything in my life was about appearances. Most of my family had never been invited to my home . . . Only my mother and father on one or two occasions. I was too afraid to be associated with the ghetto.

I did my due diligence and sent my parents money every month to help sustain them, but I did not make an effort to integrate them into my life. I did not want anyone assuming that I did not have class or feeling sorry for the "poor little ghetto girl". I had a reputation to maintain.

My mother always said, "Child, you live too far up in dem boondocks for me to drive that far. When you get done playin' Little Rich Girl, know where to find me."

My mother was a proud lady. I know she would never outright admit that I hurt her by forgetting where I came from. She thought it was easier to cut at me with her words, so we rarely spoke.

As Paris and I finished our smoked salmon and filet mignon, I could tell how hungry she was. What was most interesting was how she fed Jesse before she took a bite of anything. She gave him small portions of the fish and steak, making sure that he was taken care of before she could enjoy anything.

I watched as she carefully mashed the vegetables and food down to a consistency that he could digest. So delicately she balanced his food on her spoon and fed it to him with the utmost reverence, as if she did not know when he would have another meal. I felt a sickness in the pit of my stomach. The price of the food we were eating could possibly feed them comfortably for a few weeks.

I was starting to get annoyed with my conscience. Why was I feeling so guilty for enjoying the good life? It seemed strange that I had never pondered on how pitiful my life had become until I sat across from a younger version of myself. I knew at that point what I had to do.

I called the waiter to our table and gave him my Black Card. I had never asked the price because money was no object. That was one of the perks of being married to money. I saw Paris reach for her purse and pull out a five dollar bill and place it on the table. I almost laughed at the gesture, but I did not want to belittle her.

"Miss Claudia, thank you for the lunch and everything, but this is all I have. Can I at least leave the tip?"

Any laugh that would have left my lips stopped short at her gesture. My eyes reddened, and I felt the tears burning in my eyes. I had been hardened and numb for so long that I forgot how much a little kindness could change my whole perspective.

Paris' hand hovered over the five dollar bill, looking as if she had done something wrong by asking to leave the money. I put my hand over hers and squeezed it for reassurance.

"You know, Paris, I was just reminded of a story I heard in church one day, about a woman who gave her all. It wasn't about the amount, it was more about her heart. I could give God a million dollars, but it would not mean as much as what you just did right there."

Paris looked at me as if I had really lost all of my marbles, and the look made me smile. I felt free of constraints. I didn't care what people said or thought. I was doing what I wanted to do just because I could. And it felt SO good. I let her leave the five dollar tip because it truly meant something to her. I have always been a giver, and I believe that is why I have received so much in life.

I asked Paris if it was okay to hold Jesse, and I picked him up and carried him out of the restaurant. I tried not to think about the mess he could make on my thousand dollar suit, because I reasoned that I could always buy another one. And furthermore, Jesse was worth more than the suit.

Anyone that knew me would never have imagined that I would be out with Paris and Jesse. As much as I hated to admit it, they were growing on me. Secretly in my heart I was imagining that they were my children . . . imagining how life would have been if I had been blessed with a family of my own.

As the valet returned my car, Paris opened the door and placed Jesse in the car seat. Some of the patrons entering the restaurant gave her a second look, and I saw her unconsciously smooth her hand over her hair and straighten her clothes. I shot the patrons a dirty look and instructed Paris to have a seat. As she adjusted her seatbelt, I turned to her with a playful smile.

"Paris, have you ever been treated like a princess?" My mind was working overtime, thinking that I would make her into the daughter that I had never had. Her eyes shifted to their downward position again, and she shook her head no, as if afraid to answer. I touched her chin and directed her eyes back toward me. "Well, young lady, today is your day!"

We turned on music and smiled and sang along with the radio. I was not in reality, I was living in my own world where I was happy with my two pretend children where there was no pain, no thoughts of dying or sadness.

I took Paris to Whip It, my oldest friend's hair salon. I knew that if she was going to be my pretend daughter for the day, she had to get her head together. When we walked in, I had Paris by the hand and Jesse on my hip. I soon spotted Thelma, my stylist and best friend, and she looked as if she was about to blow a gasket.

"C.J.! Who dem kids you done picked up? Is this save the children day?" I shot her a look that said 'Girl-you-better-shut-up!', but I smiled a little and spoke in my professional voice.

"Now Thelma, you know that you have worked miracles in my hair over the years. This is Paris. Paris, this is Thelma." Thelma pulled Paris into a motherly hug and almost smothered her against her large breasts. Thelma ran her hands over Paris's head and let out a loud "Oooooooooooo!" that made Paris jump.

"Yeah, we gon' have to clear the schedule for this one! Andrey, please take this weave out so I can see what I'm workin' wit'!" Andrey was Thelma's right-hand man, only he looked more like a woman. He put out his manicured hand to take Paris' hand and I assured her that Jesse would be safe with me. As Paris sat down in Andrey's chair, Thelma took my hand and led me to the corner.

Thelma and I had grown up in the same neighborhood. We had been best friends since second grade, and no matter how 'uppity' I get, she will never let me forget who I am. She understood that with Terry, I had to live a different life. But when I was with her, she just allowed me to be me.

"Now C.J., I been knowin' you a LONG time. I ain't NEVA seen you wit' these people! Who is this girl and where did you find her?" One thing that I loved about Thelma is her inability to pretend. She was a person who said what she wanted when she wanted. That is one reason why she stayed my best friend. She always gave it to me straight.

"T., you know that I am a very sensible woman. Paris needs help. You remember what I used to look like back in the day, so don't be too quick to judge. She needs some confidence, and I know after you get a hold of that head, she will look phenomenal." Thelma smiled as if I was psyching her up, and gave me a sideways look to show me that she knew what I was trying to do.

"Okay, C.J.. She is a pretty girl. Once I am done wit' her, Chile . . . she gonna look like Beyonce's chocolate twin, okay?!" She gave me a high-five and we laughed at her craziness. I thought to myself, *I am so glad I didn't kill myself today. I sure would have missed T. and her crazy self!*

The smile vanished from Thelma's face and her tone grew somber. "Claudia, I hate to tell you this, but I saw Terry the other night at the Broadmoor Hotel walking in wit' the ho." I knew exactly who she was talkin' about, but I was tired of thinking about Terry and his mess.

"Girl, the negro had the nerve to have a hat on his big head and like he was trying to disguise himself. I know you already knew about her or I woulda straight busted him out in front of everybody. What you gonna do about him, C.J.? You can't let that man keep makin' you look like a fool!"

My mind blanked out and went back to the night she was referring to . . . it was that Tuesday before. Terry had claimed to have an out-of-town meeting that day, and said that he would most likely be home the following morning. He was gone by the time I had arrived home, as usual.

When I got to the house that day, I made a beeline toward his closet and re-counted all of his suits. The number of suits remained constant . . . 60. The only things missing were an overnight bag and some undergarments.

I started counting his clothes when I first found out about Deanna a year ago. I don't know what made me start that routine. I guess I felt somewhat in control, knowing but acting like I did not care.

Usually after his overnight escapades, he would show up with a new suit, pretending that he had a business meeting somewhere and just wanted to wear something new. And when he came back home on Wednesday, after he was asleep I went into the closet and re-counted . . . 61.

Like clockwork, Wednesday afternoon he showed up at my office with a dozen roses and a teddy bear, with a short note:

To my favorite Girl . . . 8 p.m. tonight, Onyx. Can't wait to see you.

Terry

All of the good feeling from the morning drained out of me and my mind went directly to the other woman. Deanna. The same Deanna who sent him text messages in the middle of the night. The same Deanna who was responsible for his late nights and weekend meetings. I was doing my best to deal with the infidelity. I just hated that other people knew I was being cheated on. I hated to appear weak. I wanted to keep the dignity that I had left, so I purposefully took all of the emotion off of my face and smiled at Thelma.

"Thank you for telling me, T. But I am not worried about Terry right at this moment. I am working on me." Thelma was not buying my story, and her facial expression expressed her disbelief.

"Girl, I have known you for too long. Don't play that 'tough girl' act wit' me! You know I know some people down 'round here that will bust a cap in Terry's behind and you can buy you a nice island wit' that insurance money, you hear me, Girl?" She looked dead serious, as if she had already thought about how to kill my husband and get away with it.

"All I ask is that you buy me a little villa on your island for my trouble, you know what I'm sayin'?"

I laughed so loud that it startled Jesse and he started to cry. "Oh, I'm sorry, Baby . . . I didn't mean to scare you!" I looked at Thelma as if to blame her for my outburst, and I bounced Jesse on my shoulder and walked him around the salon until he fell asleep.

I needed humor in my life. The situation was too sad to dwell on, and I was not in the mood to be depressed. Thelma made me laugh, and that day I had laughed more than I had laughed in some time. I was thankful for the joy.

Then I thought to myself, *What a sight I must be?* Me . . . dressed to the nines, holding a baby wearing tattered clothing. I must look like a bad parent. I have seen women who often looked like they spent a great deal of money on their own appearance, while their children looked as if they were poster children for the Goodwill. I purposed in my heart that if I was ever a parent, I would make sure my child had nothing but the best.

As I walked, I stopped in front of the full-length mirror. I stood there for a moment, admiring the idea of me holding my own baby. I thought about the fact that I had everything I could ever ask for at my fingertips and Paris hardly had anything of material worth. But for that moment, I would gladly trade places with her for the opportunity to be someone's mother.

I looked down at the beautiful child resting peacefully on my shoulder. Jesse was such a sweet baby . . . nine months old and so calm. As I held him, I drew off of his peace. I was reminded that a cheating husband was not the end of the world. Men cheat all the time, so what made Terry different? Why should I feel like I am the first woman in the world to get cheated on?

I let it all wash out of my brain, and I focused on life. I would enjoy the happiness that I felt with Jesse, Paris and Thelma while it lasted.

secrets

Things don't always happen in life the way that you intend them to. Lust turns into enjoyment, but can eventually lead to your whole world falling down around you.

I woke up that particular day wanting to tell Claudia the truth about what had been going on between Deanna and me. I reasoned in my mind that I was going to put it all on the table, whether she liked it or not. I was done playing around . . . I just wanted my wife back.

That day, I woke up on the couch in an awkward position. The smooth leather was somewhat discolored from my sweat and saliva and my face was contorted as my left nostril struggled to pass air.

There was a CNN anchor person on the television, discussing the current state of affairs in the Middle East. I watched as the news ticker moved across the top of the screen, and my eyes slowly focused on the time. It was nine in the morning, and I was just waking up.

I stood up to walk upstairs, needing to see Claudia. I had to release this burden from my chest and my life before it killed me. I called her name as I ran upstairs, a youthful vigor renewing me with every step.

But as I got to the top of the stairs, I remembered that Claudia had most likely left for work already. I sat down on that top step, trying to figure out how to begin the conversation about Deanna. I know what I had done was wrong, but it is not easy for me to admit my faults.

I wanted to tell her the truth, but I could not figure out just how much truth to tell her. If I told her too much, she would want to leave me. But if I told her too little, most likely she would question me until the day we died.

As I sat on that top stair, my mind recalled the final encounter that I had with Deanna the night before. She was wearing the red negligee that I had bought her from Victoria's Secret when I opened the door to go into her place. She smelled of the lavender oil she frequently massaged me with. She knew how to get me going . . . to keep me coming back.

She chose that night to claim that she was in love with me, but although she may have believed that she loved me, Deanna did not fit into my world. To my knowledge, she was only twenty-two years old and hardly polished enough to be my one and only.

To be honest, the only reasons that kept me coming back to her were her youth and her beauty. Being with her stroked my ego. I kept telling myself that she could have any man she wanted, and yet she chose me.

But after all the fun was over, I would come to realize that despite all of her appeal, she was one decision that I will regret for the rest of my life.

I should have known that I was on the wrong path by the way that I met Deanna. She was not someone I would find at church or a library, not even at the office . . . I had met her at a Gentleman's Club one evening about thirteen months ago.

It so happened that the Chairman of our Investor's Group decided to hold our monthly meeting at Stables, a well-known establishment that was famous for employing the most beautiful women in the world. I had never been there, but I had heard enough about it to be curious about what was inside. Being too curious was my first mistake.

I told myself that I could not be seen at such a place. It would be scandalous if anyone assumed that Stables was a business that I frequented. I was an active church member and I was also a public figure and very well known in my community. I relayed my concerns to the Chairman. He assured me that our meeting would be located in a remote part of the building, and we would not have contact with anyone but the other business partners.

He said that it was the only place that was available on short notice that could accommodate the room size that we needed. I took that excuse as weak, feeling that the Chairman had an ulterior motive for choosing that location.

Stables is located in a remote part of town and there were no houses or heavy traffic, just an illusion of mystery and secrecy. As I pulled up to the parking lot, I saw the vehicles of the other partners.

I sat in my car for a moment and I felt very uneasy about going in. My mind was telling me to drive away, but my curiosity was telling me to see all that I could see. I reasoned that if I decided to take a quick look but did not touch, I was safe. Plus, no one I knew from church would be in there, or at least they shouldn't be in there. Who would know if I decided to indulge myself?

My hand never left the key in the ignition, and I could have started my car and driven away without saying a word to anyone. But just as I was about to pull off, I heard a tap on my driver's side window, and I looked up to see Phil, one of the partners.

"Terry, the meeting will start in about five minutes. I can show you where to go."

Being a man of position, I could not show my apprehension. I smiled my 'power smile' and followed Phil into the building to where our meeting was being held.

I thought about how from the day I was married fifteen years ago, I had never touched another woman but Claudia. I never had to . . . Claudia is fine. She has a beautiful smile and personality, and I truly believed that she and I were made for one another. But things happen in life that make you forget what you signed up for.

While walking in to Stables, I was very apprehensive of seeing anything that could compromise my marriage. I didn't watch pornography, nor did I make a habit to flirt with other women. I may have been paranoid, but I felt as if Claudia was watching me from the walls. All through the meeting, I imagined what was going on inside of the club. I wondered what the women looked like, and as soon as a thought of another woman filled my head, I would see Claudia's beautiful face and regain focus.

As our meeting adjourned, some of the men decided to go into the club and see the women on display. I made the excuse that Claudia would be home waiting for me, and I respectfully declined their offer and headed straight to my car.

I still remember what the sky looked like that evening. The June horizon was a burnt orange with shades of purple and yellow as the sun was making its descent. I paused for a moment to focus on the sky, thinking to myself how beautifully hand-painted it appeared before me. It truly looked like God had carved the canvas of sky just for my benefit. I felt at peace with my world.

The weather was so beautiful that day that I had decided to drive my convertible Boxster S Black Edition Porsche. I knew that I turned heads in my car, and my ego was stroked each time someone looked in awe in my direction.

As I rounded to the passenger side, I saw Deanna for the first time. She was standing with her back against the wall and her face in her hands. She had been crying softly, and as a man I felt it was my duty to make sure she was okay. I walked closer to her.

"Hey, are you okay?"

She raised her head and looked at me with the most beautiful smoky grey eyes I had ever seen. Her skin reminded me of butterscotch candy, and her jeans hugged her curves and made me take notice.

"Yeah, I'm okay." She spoke with a coarseness to her voice that indicated she had been crying for some time.

"You don't look okay," I said, coming closer. I had the strangest feeling being next to her. It was as if I could feel the heat coming off of my body as I moved in closer to her.

She woke up all of the negative feelings I felt about my marriage, thinking about all of the areas that Claudia was deficient. I instantly noticed my attraction toward Deanna, and was sure she could feel what her presence was doing to me. The man who was afraid to even look at a woman was replaced by a lust-filled man who threw caution out the window.

I saw her eyes scan over me, and I could see her erase the vulnerability from her eyes as her sex-appeal turned on.

"You think you can make me okay?" She asked me the question with a soft 'purr' to her voice. She was so brazen and full of confidence that it threw me off. I had heard about women like her, but had never been in a position with a woman as forward as she was. I was used to women come on to me because of my status, but when they did it was with a slight reverence.

Deanna was a different breed. She looked at me as if we were familiar. She knew she was beautiful and she was not shy with her beauty. I felt mesmerized by her. Her eyes kept roaming over my body like she wanted to devour me, and I walked right into her seduction.

My mind spoke loudly to me, reminding me of what I had to lose if I didn't nip this woman in the bud . . . my reputation, my dignity and my wife possibly. I believed that if Claudia knew that I was having an inappropriate conversation with another woman, she would nail me to the wall.

But as I looked at Deanna, a beautiful sexy woman . . . I was reminded of how I felt the first time I laid eyes on Claudia. I felt the desire to touch her and hold her, even though I knew it would be wrong.

One thought that plagued my mind was how quickly she turned on the 'sexy' act. She had just been crying one moment, and the next, she was being sexually suggestive. It was as if she knew what I wanted, and she could switch back to her role with not even a moment's notice.

As she stood up straight, I noticed the fullness of her breasts, the curve of her hips and the juiciness of her lips. I felt as if I was falling under a spell. Her eyes were pulling me in to her clutches, but I can't blame it all on her. I wanted to be taken.

From that day, her agenda was not hidden and against my better judgment, we exchanged numbers. I knew that Claudia did not go through my phone, so I figured giving her my number would not be an issue.

We started off with text messages. Initially, they were harmless, but after the first couple of days, our communication had turned very explicit. I did not have a horrible marriage, but I focused on the negative parts of it to make myself feel better about what I was doing. I gave the excuse that Claudia was boring in bed and that our love life had declined over the years.

The more negative I portrayed Claudia, the more Deanna compensated. She progressed from sending explicit text messages to sending me racy pictures. The newness and excitement made me grow bolder and more pronounced with my requests. She did not say 'No', and although I knew better, neither did I.

After the first week of knowing her, Deanna had invited me to her apartment and we became intimate. With all of the texting, I knew that something was bound to happen. I just did not expect it to happen that soon.

In the beginning, I was overly paranoid. Every day I saw Claudia, I thought she would suddenly tell me that I was busted or try to kill me. But as time progressed and I figured out that I could get away with it, I became less concerned with getting caught and more focused on the pleasure.

It was nothing for me to lie to Claudia . . . she seemed as if she did not care what I did anymore. I reasoned that Claudia was busy with her work anyway, so she would not miss me if I was gone a few nights.

As the sexual relationship grew between Deanna and me, all intimacy with Claudia ceased. I felt guilty about it in the beginning, but Claudia started to work more so I figured she didn't want to sleep with me anyway. Besides, Deanna was willing to do any and everything that I asked, no matter how demeaning or far-fetched.

In return for her body, I paid her rent and bought her whatever she wanted. I had moments where I felt pathetic, as if she was just my personal prostitute. But whenever she would sense that I was feeling uncertain, she would tell me how much she needed, appreciated and loved me. In my heart, I knew it was all an act.

But it still felt good to hear it.

I was a forty year old man, and I still had the power to attract someone like her. She made me feel good about myself. No matter how much money I had or what position I held, it was nice to hear someone say that they desired me.

In all of my excitement, I was starting to despise myself. I used to be a man of character, who did the right thing, even when no one was looking. My father taught me that it was important to live a disciplined life. I was taught to honor my wife and myself. I was raised to be a good, Christian man.

Somehow during the affair, I stopped listening to my conscience. I became content doing what felt right, versus what was right. I had elevated myself to a place where nothing that I did was wrong, because being with Deanna had convinced me that I was a man with money and power, so the world was mine. I started to behave as if those things made me a god.

With all of the lies and secrets, everything changed the night that Deanna told me she loved me. For the first time in our affair, I could tell that she really meant it. Our thing had started as fun and had turned into something serious. I started to panic because Deanna had fallen in love, and that was not part of the plan. As much as I desired her, I did not love her. I only woman that I had ever loved was Claudia.

With that realization, I thought about the events of the past year and questioned myself. How could I claim to love someone and cheat on them at the same time? How could I love her and make love to someone else? Every time had sex with Deanna, I was potentially putting Claudia at risk. Yes, I used condoms, but nothing is one hundred percent effective.

I thought about what Claudia's face would look like when she heard the news. She would probably be angry or cry, and I did not want to see her in either state. I was sure that she suspected something, since she and I have not been intimate in some time.

On the days when I felt that I should at least try to perform like a husband, I have tried to touch her, only to be rejected. So I decided to stop trying. I convinced myself that I was only having the affair because Claudia didn't want to sleep with me.

I would come in late and sleep on the couch, or sleep in a guest room. In public, we would talk and maintain the appearance of the perfect couple, all the while living like strangers in our home. We would go to church every Sunday, sitting next to each other on the pew, playing our parts. Sadly . . . we would only be close on Sundays. There would be times I would go days without actually seeing or talking to Claudia.

After a while, we fell into the routine of only being a public couple. She did not ask questions about what I did, and I never asked her questions. We lived in the same house, and only talked on a need-to basis.

Despite what was going on at home, hearing Deanna tell me that she loved me slapped me back into reality. Hearing her say that she loved me made me remember that I already had someone to love at home. I knew that I had to stop playing house with Deanna.

I had my epiphany as I was laying naked on my mistress's bed at 11:12 p.m. I sat up straight and felt as if the weight of the world landed on my head. The pride, ego and selfishness made way for a wave of guilt that enveloped me, and I looked at Deanna with sternness on my face while watching her loving expression fade.

"Look Deanna, you know what this was. I liked what I had with you, but I am never leaving my wife." With that, I stood up and started to put my clothes back on.

"Oh, okay . . . so let me make sure I understand this." A crazy look came over Deanna, and she rose up to stand within inches of my face.

"So you tellin' me that I'm good enough for you to sleep with, but not good enough for you to be with? You come and sex me up then think you can throw me away like that?"

I surveyed the room quickly to see where possible weapons might be. The way she was talking and looking, I did not know what to expect from her. I tried to speak calmly as I moved slowly toward the door.

"Deanna, look at me. I never promised you anything but what I gave you. I never implied that I had any plans to be anything more than a sexual partner and a financier. I am sure you are aware that this had to come to an end at some point."

I tried to avoid her eyes, because I did not want to know what she was feeling. I just wanted to get my stuff and walk away as if none of this every happened. I was prepared to try and forget about Deanna, and go back to Claudia and resume life as normal. What came out of her mouth was worse than anything I could have imagined.

She laid back on the bed, with one leg stretched forward and the other leg bent with the sole of her foot resting firmly on the mattress. She remained completely naked as she pulled out a cigarette from the nightstand next to the bed.

Until that moment, I had never known that she smoked. I would come to understand that there was a lot that I did not know about Deanna.

"You think you are so smart and you have it all together."   As she spoke, her tongue curled wisps of smoke around it until the smoke curled and drifted upward toward the ceiling.   Her voice had taken on a different accent, slightly Spanish.   She sounded angry and tired.

My eyes followed the trail of white nicotine as it ascended toward the heavens, dancing its way in a smooth, fluid stream up until it disappeared from sight. She slowly inhaled the white cigarette with blue lines curving around the filter.

I had a feeling that whatever she was going to say was going to leave me with a sickening feeling. I made a motion to walk toward the door, but her voice caught me in mid-step.

"Do you remember the first day we met? I saw you when you first reached the parking lot. I smelled money all over you, Papi . . . from your Movado watch to your Ralph Lauren loafers. And the car! The car was a definite give away. You didn't walk like a regular person. You walked like the world was yours."

I felt an anger burn in the pit of my stomach, realizing that I had been a target from the beginning. She had set me up, but there was nothing I could do about it.

"I knew from the moment I saw you that I was going to make you my Sugar Daddy. I purposefully waited outside by your car, ready to turn on the waterworks. And you fell for it, like the sucker you are."

She laughed an evil laugh, one that caught me in a state of utter disbelief. This was the same woman I risked my marriage for? I made a move toward the door, never to see her again.

But as quickly as I was heading toward the door, she ran up and held it shut, throwing herself on me.

"I thought I would have a few sessions with you and get a little money. I never intended to fall in love with you, Daddy. You are the perfect man . . . I could make you so happy. I want to be with you forever, and have your children. We could have the perfect life."

She started to kiss me, and my defenses waned. I found myself putting my arms around her again, but my conscience kept saying "No". I could sense her desperation as she molded her body into mine, hoping that her sex appeal was enough to keep me from leaving.

Over and over and over I heard the word "No" in my head, until the word finally spilled out over my lips.

"No, Deanna. I can't do this anymore. I WON'T do this anymore." I tried to untangle myself from her arms, but she would not let me go.

"So what am I supposed to do now?" She yelled at the top of her lungs, giving me an Oscar worthy performance. "Do I just walk away from this like I never knew you? How could you do this to me?"

The events of the past year flashed before my eyes. The affair had gotten so out of control. I felt like the lowest person on the face of the Earth. Not only was I about to hurt my wife, I was hurting Deanna as well.

"Deanna, I am sorry. I truly am. But if I have a choice whether to hurt you or her, I owe it to her to stop doing this with you. She didn't deserve this." I kept my voice stone-cold and even, but I could not meet Deanna's gaze.

"Fine then."

Her face straightened up as she drained all trace of emotion from it. Her posture became erect and all indications of love were replaced with fiery, hateful looks.

"Go back home to your boring life and play house with your sexless wife. You think that you ain't gonna cheat on her again? If you ain't getting it from here, you gonna get it from somewhere, Daddy. Mark my words."

Her words were stinging in my ears, but I kept walking toward the door. I could not believe everything that I had risked, and it was all for sex. I kept my stride as I put my hand on the front door and opened it. When Deanna realized that I was not going to be back, she held the door open wider for me to walk out.

"Do you think that I won't be able to find another man in a heartbeat? It was nice knowin' ya." And with that, Deanna pushed me out of her door and out of her life.

I felt a weight lifted off of me, and yet I felt a sadness come over me. I would miss Deanna. She made me feel alive again. But I knew in my heart that love was not always about a 'feeling'. Love has to be a choice.

My mind drifted back to Claudia, and I mentally set up scenarios on how I was going to get back into her good graces. I drove back home in a hurry. When I got inside, I rushed up the stairs only to find that Claudia was not in bed.

I walked through the upper level, searching every room hoping to catch sight of her. As I reached the last room, the room we had initially planned to use for a baby room, I saw her laid on the floor.

There was a bottle of Ambien laid out by her feet, and she was snoring quite loudly as if she had mistakenly fallen in that spot. I had never known Claudia to take prescription medication to be able to sleep and I wondered how many nights she performed this ritual.

"Claudia, I am home. Come to bed." I made a motion to help her off of the floor, and she looked at me with a sad expression on her face.

"I am fine, Terry. I would like to sleep right here." She laid her head back down on the pillow that she brought into the room. The room smelled of sadness and despair, and I wanted to run away. As I tried to pull the covers up around her chin, she pulled covers closer to her body and yelled, "I said I'M FINE!"

I retreated from the room unsure of what to do next. I was finally prepared to be a good husband, and she was not giving me the opportunity. I felt like I needed to reconcile things immediately, because I was not sure that I would have the nerve to do it another day. Apparently, it would take more than just one night to fix it.

I opted to turn on the TV and lay on the couch until I could talk with her in the morning, but because I had overslept, I decided to get ready and take her somewhere special for lunch to talk to her.

I couldn't wait to see my wife again and tell her that I loved her.

change

When Paris came out of the salon, she hardly resembled the girl I had met that morning. Her hair was styled and beautifully layered, and she looked more beautiful than even she imagined.

I paused a moment before we entered the car, so that I could get my emotions in check. I felt like a proud mother. Paris was giddy, constantly touching her soft hair as if she could not believe that it was actually hers. I caught her looking at herself in the side mirrors, then looking back at me.

"Paris, I would like to take you to Macy's to get a few outfits for you and Jesse. Your shoes . . . ," I pause for a moment, unable to keep speaking. I remembered what it was like to be the girl in the room that was the worst dressed and self-conscious.

Paris turned and gazed out of the window, and we rode in silence for a while. I played with the radio again, pushing buttons to keep busy, when all the while my mind was flooded with thoughts.

We reached the mall and I told her that she could have whatever she wanted. I watched her excitedly, going from section to section, looking at things she could not previously afford.

By the time we were through, she and Jesse had clothes to last them for days. She looked beautiful, and I know that she felt beautiful. I felt her level of confidence shoot through the roof as she walked through the mall, holding bags from Macy's and Sacs Fifth Avenue.

As we left the mall, I still had questions burning in my mind. Initially, I planned to just do something nice for Paris and Jesse . . . to make it a day that she would never forget. With each passing minute, I found myself growing attached to her. I wanted a family of my own for so long. With Terry and me, the possibility was gone. I wanted to enjoy the feeling for as long as possible.

"So why ain't you got no kids?" Paris's voice broke me from my thoughts. I thought about the question for a moment before I answered, because the subject always made me a little emotional.

"Well . . . my husband and I wanted to wait for the right time before we started having children. When we were finally ready to have kids, we found out that we weren't able to have any."

We drove in silence for a while, lost in our own thoughts. I was starting to feel sorry for myself again, thinking about my missed opportunities. As my mind became cloudy, I decided to pull off of the main road so that we could talk.

I turned on my blinker to ease into a parking lot, and I noticed we were right back where we had started this morning. We were in the McDonald's parking lot, but I was looking at a much different girl when I looked at Paris.

"Paris?" My voice cracked a little as I called her name, hesitant to ask the question that burned like bile in the back of my throat. I turned in my seat to look her in her eyes.

"Paris, you are under no obligation to tell me anything. I have not done things for you today just to gain access into your personal life."

I paused a moment before proceeding, unsure of how she would react to my question. She did not seem like the type of girl to yell or catch an attitude, but in all actuality I had only known her for some hours. I had no idea what she was capable of.   I realized that I had a habit of overthinking things, so I decided to just ask the question.

"Paris, why are you and Jesse living in a shelter?" She let out a slow breath, as if she had been waiting for me to ask that question the entire time we were together. She stared straight ahead, seemingly watching the story unfold before her.

"I ain't from here Miss Claudia, if you can't tell. I came here 'cause I met somebody online about a year and a half ago . . . this dude named Calvin." She looked down at her hands and started to rub them together, her fingers trembling.

"I just wanted to get away! You know, my Mama got eight kids. We was all livin' in the projects and since I was the oldest, she just figured I was 'sposed to take care of everybody while she did what she wanted to. He told me I could come down here and he would take care o' me, so I said I'd come.

"He had his own place and a job and told me that he could help me get in school and stuff. He bought me a bus ticket and I came down here. But when I got here, he was different."

I inwardly braced myself, knowing that what she was about to tell me something that was going to make me want to go find this Calvin and beat his socks off. But I did not interrupt. I just let her keep talking.

"He had a job and a place and stuff, but he was crazy. He was drinkin' and smokin' weed all the time. When I got pregnant with Jesse, I couldn't go nowhere. I wasn't goin' back home to my Mama, and Calvin knew that.

"So after I had Jesse he just started actin' more crazy. One day his friend came over and he thought I was lookin' at him like I wanted him. He held me down and beat me wit' a belt. Then he burned me wit' cigarettes all up my arms and told me I better not look at another man or try to leave him or he was gonna kill me."

She lifted up the arms of her shirt and showed me the trails of burn mark scars. I instantly felt sick, and I wanted to kill Calvin and every man like him. Then I thought how funny it was that I was willing to fight for Paris, but not even for my own self.

"One night when he was passed out from drinkin', I had to sneak out the apartment in the middle of the night wit' Jesse, and went to the shelter. I figured we

be better in the street than to have him beatin'
on me. I seen it happen too many times wit'
my Mama. I can't let my son see me gettin'
beat up."

She shook her head back and forth as
hot tears fell quickly from her eyes. She may
have looked a mess before I met her, but she
possessed something that I was missing from
my own life, and that was strength. I had all
of my needs met, I lived in a million-dollar
home with foreign cars and jewelry. People
looked at me and thought that I had it all
together.

The truth was . . . I was weak and that
realization slapped me in my face. This girl
had the strength to leave Calvin in the middle
of the night, to sneak away with her child not
knowing what the future held. She only had
the faith that she could make it.

"You know, Paris . . . you have truly inspired me today. Here I was feeling all sorry for myself, and you have been through Hell. Forgive me."

I felt honored that she trusted me enough to tell me her story. In the moment that she opened up to me, I knew that we were bonded together. We were both learning to let our guard down.

I started the car and we made our way back to the highway. I almost jumped when I heard the telephone ringing. I saw that it was a call from Terry, and I stared at the number in bewilderment. Terry hardly ever called me during the day. I answered the phone and held it in disbelief.

"Hel . . . hel . . . hello?" I am sure he heard the questioning tone in my voice, and wondered what was going on.

"Claudia, I stopped by your office to see you this afternoon, and your secretary told me that you called in for today. Is something wrong?"

I could detect a slight panicked tone to his voice, which caused me to feel all the more unsure about his phone call. He rarely came to my office, so that was another strange occurrence. My suspicions grew even greater.

"Nothing is wrong Terry. I just decided to spend the day doing something more important." I turned and looked at Paris and smiled, and she smiled a genuine smile of appreciation toward me.

"Where are you at Claudia? Who are you with?" He yelled into the receiver and I let out a soft nonchalant laugh, dismissing his questions. "Terry, I can't remember you ever asking me such questions."

"I just really need to talk to you. Can we meet tonight for dinner?" Red flags were going up all around my head, but I needed to play it cool with him. I would not let him detect any emotion.

"Sure. Our usual place? Is 8 okay?" I heard him hesitate slightly, but he responded that eight would be fine. I could not disconnect that call fast enough.

"Is dat yo' husband? He sound all proper . . . is he white?" I laughed so hard that I almost lost control of the wheel. "No, Paris. He is not white. He has just been raised to speak in a very proper manner."

"Well I hope one day I meet a rich, white man who can show me what it's like to be rich." I remember thinking that money was the end-all-to-be-all. Money could buy you a lot of things, but not happiness.

"I am obligated to inform you that there are men of all races who are wealthy. And in reality, there are good and bad men in every race. You just pray that God blesses you with a good man. Don't be so concerned with his color OR his wallet."

I thought back to when I first met Terry. We both attended the same school, and I was a Freshman in college and he was a Senior. Terry was the guy that everyone knew and liked but secretly hated. He had it all . . . popularity, looks and money. I, on the other hand, had a father who was the neighborhood alcoholic and a mother who worked a minimum of two jobs to keep our home together.

Terry's family had generations of wealth, and mine was from the bottom. We were a prime example of 'haves' and 'have-nots'. He would never turn his back on family, so in order for us to survive as a couple, I had to turn my back on mine.

"You said you were looking for a sitter for Jesse, correct?" Paris looked at me with a sad expression.

"I need to so I can find a job and start school, but I don't know who crazy and who ain't. I can't just leave him with anybody." I realized that if Paris wanted to get somewhere in life, she was definitely going to have to work on her vocabulary.

"Well, today is your lucky day. I happen to know one of the best baby sitters in town. And I am sure we can work out a deal with her, she will take care of Jesse like he is her own."

As much as I did not want to see her, I knew my mother was the best person to help Paris. My mother had decided to start her own daycare business after my father started having kidney problems. I guess that all of the alcohol had taken its' toll on his body and his body decided to rebel against the abuse.

So as always, my mother stepped in and arranged her life around him so that he could be comfortable. I believe that even if he was a crackhead, she would have stayed by his side and made excuses for his drug abuse.

As we pulled up in front of my parent's house, I saw the children playing on plastic toys in the backyard. All of the children looked so happy and peaceful, just like I was at that age.

I saw my mother standing on the side of the house looking the same as she had the last time I saw her. She was putting out her Kool cigarette, her hair smoothed back into a bun. She was still slim and pretty, but she always looked tired . . . maybe the result of years of running behind a no-good man.

I thought about the relationship I had with my mother over the past fifteen years since I had married Terry. I remembered his mother taking me into a room the night that she met my family at our wedding rehearsal dinner.

"Claudia," she said as she smoothed out her satin dress, "I know that you cannot help who birthed you and since Terry decided to marry you despite my concerns, I expect you to conduct yourself like a Brixton. I will give you this piece of advice . . . if you want to become one of us, disassociate yourself from those 'ghetto folk' you call family. I won't have them being a reflection on me."

I remember feeling so ashamed of my family at that point. I felt like I could not let them stop me from becoming a part of a family that I idolized. I needed to be with Terry. He was my ticket out of the ghetto.

So in the end, I chose Terry over my family. When my mother noticed me, she looked at me like I was a stranger. I am sure that Paris could sense my hesitation, but there was no way to hide the feelings between myself and my mother.

"The prodigal daughter has returned. It must be my lucky day." She flicked her cigarette over the fence in a nearby yard. "You ain't neva' jus' showed up like this! And you got a friend wit' you, too!"

I wanted to take Paris' hand and walk back to my car and drive far, far away. I know that my mother had never forgiven me for choosing Terry over her, so I could not shy away from her resentment. However, I knew my mother well enough to know that she could be professional when it came to work. She would not take her anger toward me out on Jesse.

"Hello, Mother. This is Paris. Paris, this is my mother, Ida Mae." My mother looked at me like she wanted to slap the teeth out of my mouth.

"I ain't never heard-a no black chile callin' they Mama, 'Mother'. Paris, you call me Ms. Ida or you can call me Mama Mae. Don't call me Mother. I hate that crap."

I straightened up my face and remembered my 'Brixton-stone-cold-façade'. My mother did not want to acknowledge that I was not the same little girl she raised. I was a wealthy, educated lady now. I was not going to talk back to her . . . I knew she would slap my teeth out of my mouth if I ever thought I could talk back, regardless of my educational level.

"Mom, I just wanted to bring someone by to meet the best baby-sitter in the country."

My mom took one look at Paris and pulled her into a warm embrace. She held her and rocked her back and forth like a mom was supposed to. I felt a tinge of jealousy, remembering what it was like to be held by my mother. I also felt sadness, realizing what I had given up in life for Terry.

"Mom, Paris needs a sitter for little Jesse here. She will be going to school and she needs someone she can trust to watch him for her. Do you have any openings?"

That day, my mom showed me that although she was not the most eloquent person, she had a good heart. She showed me that despite your status, you can always be kind.

"I would be more than happy to keep this handsome young man. Why don't you come inside and have some tea wit' me, and tell me all about him."

My mother and Paris went inside of the house and I stayed outside for a while to mentally put my day together. I stood against the fence and sank my Christian Louboutin suede heels in the soft mud outlying the sidewalk. I felt the shoes depreciate with every particle of dirt that attached itself to them.

I didn't care.

I looked at the house Terry had purchased for my parents. It was better than anything that we had ever lived in for the duration of my childhood. I guess that is why I felt okay with giving up on my family. I reasoned that since I could not associate with them, I would try to buy them a little piece of happiness.

I watched the children play outside with Geri, my mother's assistant. I must have fallen into a daze when I heard a voice behind me.

"So Miss Thang, you gonna tell me what's up, or will I hear 'bout it on the news." I had heard that a mother's intuition was beyond comprehension. She may not be presented with all of the facts, but inside I knew that she knew. Although I did not want to give her the satisfaction of watching me fall, I did not care what she thought. I was done putting on a front.

"I don't really feel like talking about it, Mom. Let's just say I am tired."

Surprisingly, my mom did not say a word. She just stood a distance away from me, pulling her pack of Kools from her shirt pocket. I watched her light up a cigarette and inhale deeply. When she started to talk, the smoke floated out of her mouth at the same time as her words.

"I knew one day you was gon' see fa' yo'self. You pushed us to tha' corner like we wasn't nothin' cause we was poor. You gave us a lotta stuff ova' tha years and I am thankful. But you didn't haveta do me like that, Child. You didn't haveta . . ."

My mother turned her back to me and I felt so low. I could not remember the last time I had seen my mother cry. I thought that she was so tough, but I saw that she was the one who taught me how to push my emotions to the bottom and keep moving forward.

"Mom, I am sorry. I didn't think about your feelings and I'm sorry. But to be honest with you, today is not about me. It's about Paris and Jesse. I can't help myself, so I thought I may as well help someone else."

She straightened up her face and her clothes. "Well, I suppose you right. We can talk about our crap another day."

I felt disappointed in myself for being so short with my mother. I know that she had things that she wanted to say to me, and I had not given her the opportunity to say before. However, I did not feel strong enough emotionally to have that talk with her yet.

"You have my word that I won't keep being a stranger, Mom. Today I would really love if you could help Paris with her situation. Can you please help her?" She dropped her cigarette to the pavement and stomped it out with her house-shoe. She continued talking as if she had not heard my question.

"I worried 'bout you for a while, Chile. I thought you was so worried about money that you wasn't gonna remember you is still my girl. I prayed that God wouldn't let me lose you. He ain't let me down yet."

I followed behind her, letting her words sink in. She still thought of me as her 'Girl', even though I did not treat her like my 'Mama'.

We stepped inside of the house and I let my mother make arrangements with Paris for Jesse's childcare, and informed her that I would be paying for it.

I could not look my mother in the face as I was leaving. I did not trust myself to speak to her. She stood on the porch and watched as we fastened Jesse in his car seat. She watched as my car disappeared down the street, the same smile resting on her lips until she was no longer visible in my rearview mirror.

"You and yo' Mom is good people, but she don't seem like she would be your Mom." I knew what she meant by her statement, but I wanted her to explain what she meant by it.

"What do you mean?" I left the question in the air as she took a moment to gather her thoughts.

"I don't know. I guess I just thought you came from some rich, stuck up folks. People who talked more like yo' husband. Yo' mama talk more like me." Her perception was one of the main reasons why I felt I had to keep my distance. I wanted to be looked at as someone distinguished and important, not some ghetto refugee.

"You know, Paris, my mother always had my back, and she always pushed for me to be the best in everything that I did. I was foolish enough to think that money would make me happy, but I forgot how much my mother meant. I would trade everything that I own right now to have a family and love."

"Miss Claudia, I know it's not everything. But when you ain't got nothin', it's a lot. You drivin' a nice car, you can do whatever you want whenever you want. I wanna be sittin' like you one day."

Hearing her words, I felt saddened. People see the glitter and gold on the outside, but they don't see the loneliness. I had valuable things, but I did not possess much of anything priceless.

"Paris, you can do above and beyond anything that I have accomplished in life if you keep God first. Don't think that a man will define you. Know your worth. We have one more stop to make and then I will let you go, Sweetie."

I felt the mood shift in the car, and Jesse must have felt it, too. I heard him stir in the backseat, seemingly feeding off of his mother's despair.

That day I had shown her a world she had never seen before. I had given her a new look, new clothes and safety. But she had to return to her real world, and in that world, there were no fancy restaurants and shopping sprees. She did not have anyone driving her around in a luxury car. She didn't even have a home.

"Miss Claudia, I ain't never had no one be this nice to me, just to be nice. I ain't never gonna forget what you done for us. Thank you so much."

I did not respond to her words. I maintained my silence until we reached the address that meant so much to me.

5879 Cypress Lane.

Before us was a brick house, with a nice manicured lawn. A beautiful wooden fence encased the yard that led to a sprawling wooden porch with a wicker chair on it.

"Please come with me, Paris. I would like to show you something." As Paris exited the car, she looked at the house in awe, commenting on its beauty.

I took her inside and showed her around, making her familiar with every room. She told me that she had never been in a house that looked similar to it, and I remembered how I felt when I first bought it. The little brick house was nothing compared to the house that Terry and I lived in, or the house that he had grown up in. However, it was the first house that I purchased myself.

"Paris, this was my first house that I ever bought with my own money. I own a few rental properties, but I had not found anyone that I felt suited this house. I want to give it to you and Jesse."

Paris started to shake her head 'No' and proceeded to walk backward away from me. Needless to say, I was confused by her actions, and she could tell by the puzzled look on my face that I was unsure why she was declining my offer. I wanted to give her the house . . . I needed to give it to her.

"Miss Claudia, I don't have no job. I don't have no money. I can't afford . . ."

I know that Terry would have told me I was an idiot for giving her a house, but I smiled my knowing smile and said to her sweetly, "I am not asking you to rent it. I am giving it to you. I will pay the utilities for the next six months until you get settled, and then they will be your responsibility. There is a bus line that comes close, so you will have transportation. The only thing I ask is that you get enrolled in college and finish. That is the only repayment that I want."

Paris looked at me as if I had really lost my mind. The song from that morning started playing in my head again .

Maybe I'm crazy . . .

I could not stop my laugh. I had finally lost my last piece of good mind and it felt soooooo goooood! Jesse caught on and started laughing himself, and finally Paris joined in and we all laughed until we cried . . . with no one really knowing why they were laughing or crying. As the tears started flowing, the gravity of what had happened dawned on Paris.

"I got a house . . . me an' Jesse got a HOUSE . . . THANK YOU, JESUS!" She screamed at the top of her lungs and started to dance around the kitchen, holding a joyful Jesse on her hip. She held him close to her tear-stained face and chanted "WE GOT A HOUSE" over and over until she melted on the floor in a big pile of gratitude. I did not try to stop her . . . I just admired her freedom from a distance.

I felt that day was the beginning of my rebirth. In the midst of my pain, God showed me how to be selfless. My moment of weakness led to a lifetime of gift to someone else.

I really started to think about my life as of late, and before I knew it I thought to myself, "Thank you, Terry, for messing up!" As soon as the thought left my head, I had to re-harness that thought.

I was crazy . . . but I wasn't that crazy.

I ordered Paris and Jesse a pizza and assured her that I would be back the next day to take her to the store to get groceries and house supplies. All of the rooms were furnished with bedding, and she had everything that she needed.

She and Jesse had clothes from our earlier shopping spree. She hugged me tight and did not let me go for what seemed like five minutes. I was thankful that I had the opportunity to bless someone's life.

As I left Paris and Jesse, I realized that I had to go back to reality myself where life was not all fun.   I had some real situations to address.

Before I headed home to get ready for dinner with Terry, I had one final stop to make. I drove to the familiar address, walked up to the front door and knocked, unafraid to confront the source of my pain.

When she answered the door, I saw that she was wearing the same negligée that she had on the night before. The smell of heavy smoke met me when I opened the door.

"Can I help you?" She asked me the question with heavy eyes, looking me over completely before opening her door too far.

"Hello Deanna. I have been waiting for some time to speak with you." She opened her door a little more, as if to gauge who she was speaking with. She looked annoyed that I knew her on a first name basis.

"Do I know you, Lady?" I resisted the urge to drag her out by her hair.

"You know me by way of my husband, Terry. Apparently, you have been sleeping with him for some time."

Deanna smiled and opened the door completely to allow me to walk in. I came in and looked around her living room and I instantly thought of Terry sitting on her couch, touching her . . . the thought of him being intimate with this woman made me not want to touch anything.

I felt as if I was in a Western movie and she and I were about to take twenty paces and shoot. We looked each other over, not making any attempt to hide our expressions.

"So you are the infamous Wifey." She walked around me, continuing to look at me from head to toe. "Why are you here? Shouldn't you be out keeping your husband happy instead of wasting time talking to me?"

I have never been a fighter, but I had to resist the urge. The nerve of that woman . . .

"I am just here to give you a warning. I have tolerated your little affair for too long, but now I'm telling you that you need to stay away from my husband. The next time I won't be so nice."

She did not react in fear . . . she merely laughed at me. She looked at me as if I was worthless, holding her stomach dramatically as if her laughter made it hard for her to stand up straight.

"Don't come up in my house tellin' me nothin', Chica. If you were more of a woman your husband would have no need of me. He wanted a REAL woman, Mami. You ain't enough for him."

She stared me down, looking for a reaction. Her words hit me like a bullet in my heart and I wondered if this was how Terry really felt inside. I felt deflated and was sorry that I had even stopped at her house but I knew that I could not show any sign of weakness.

"Any woman who would sleep with a married man is a pitiful creature who needs prayer. He is MY husband!" By that time I was yelling and advancing on her, ready to strike.

"You women crack me up . . . always so quick to run to the woman your husband is cheating with. You wanna fight me, Mami? Go 'head! But at the end of the day, your husband is still gonna be out lookin' to get it from somebody."

I felt like I was in a world of make-believe again, and that all of my air was gone. I looked at her as if seeing her for the first time.

"You know, Deanna . . . you are absolutely right. I apologize for stopping over here . . . I don't know what I was thinking. I thought maybe if you saw me you would see that I am a good woman and a good person and that I did not deserve to be cheated on. Maybe I hoped to change your mind."

I turned my back to her and walked to the door, willing myself not to break down. I felt dejected and humiliated, but I kept my head high. Before I was completely out of the door, I turned around and looked at her. The words that I said caused her to smile a smile of satisfaction.

"If it means anything, Mami, you are a lot prettier than I had imagined. I expected you to be old and fat and boring. But for the right price, I can teach you how to keep your man. Then you won't have to worry about chicks like me."

Terry was so stupid. All that woman wanted was a dollar bill, and I am sure he spent a substantial amount of them on her.

"So besides sex, what did you get out of the arrangement? Did he love you?"

Deanna paused a moment before speaking, as if she had to get her story straight before speaking to me.

"He bought me stuff, and yeah, he just told me last night that he was in love with me. But I don't do love. I am all about the money."

I felt my anger rising up for both him and her. I felt as if throughout the whole stupid affair, I was the one who paid the price. I was fed up, so I told her the words that she was longing to hear.

"Thank you for time, Deanna. You can have him."

honesty

I have heard it said countless times that women want an honest man. I was starting to believe that it was all a lie perpetuated by some woman to get a man to tell his business. Not all women can handle the truth. Claudia, however, was a different breed of woman. After fifteen years of marriage, I thought that I knew her inside and out.

Claudia was a very time conscious person. If I said that I would meet her somewhere at seven o'clock, she would undoubtedly be there ten minutes early, waiting for me to arrive.

When I arrived at The Onyx, I noticed that she was not there yet. I looked at my watch, which read 7:55 p.m. I thought it was odd for me to be at dinner before her. I was seated at the best table as I uncomfortably waited alone.

By the time the clock showed 8:15 p.m., I picked up my phone ready to call and make sure that she was not in an accident. As soon as I had the phone in my hand, I saw her.

I almost did not recognize her because she looked like a model. Her hair was down and flowing, she had on a tight cocktail dress that fit perfectly. Usually she was dressed like an executive, but that night she looked like a woman . . . a vibrant, confident and sexy woman.

I saw more than a few heads turn as she walked across the room. I did not know what had gotten into her, but I could not stop admiring her. She looked so beautiful that I was almost hesitant to tell her about Deanna. I started to think selfishly . . . strategizing on how I could get her to make love to me before I let the cat out of the bag.

"Claudia, you look stunning. I almost didn't recognize you. What did you do to your hair? You look so good in that dress." She looked down at her clothes and touched her face in a dramatic fashion.

"I do look beautiful, don't I? I have never felt so beautiful in my life. Thank you." She adjusted her napkin and spread it across her thighs, all the while making sure that I noticed how short her skirt was. Not to mention her beautiful legs . . .

"I can't even tell you the last time I remember you telling me I looked beautiful, or nice, or saying anything that resembled a compliment toward me." She was burning holes in my face with her eyes, making me feel uncomfortable.

"So what was it that you needed to talk to me about, Terry?" All playfulness was gone from her voice. She sounded as if she was building up her protective wall before I could say anything to damage her.

A wave of guilt flooded over me. I had been practicing my speech all day . . . how I planned to tell her about the infidelity. Only when I was looking at her face, I felt the shame in my words.

"Claudia, I don't even know how to begin. I thought we could talk in here since it is a familiar place, but I am not sure that this is the right atmosphere for what I need to tell you. Would you mind if we went outside?"

I did not think through what her possible show of emotion may be. I cared about her feelings, but I was trying to open up for my own benefit.

"Terry, I know that whatever you plan to tell me will not be pleasant. You know that I am not the type to cause a scene, so please just say whatever it is you need to say so it can be done."

For all of her bravado, I noticed a slight tremble in her voice. She wanted to appear tough, but she was afraid. Since we were both in an awkward emotional position, I just let it spill out.

"Claudia, I have been having an affair for the past year. I am sorry . . . I am sure you did not expect me to tell you this, but don't worry, It's completely over. I just . . ."

My words trailed off as I saw the blank expression on her face. There were no yells, no tears, no words . . . nothing. She just looked out of the window as if she was bored and had not heard a word that I said.

"Did you hear me Claudia? I said that I . . ."

"Had an affair. I heard you, Terry. Is that all that you had to tell me?" She was staring at me, daring me to turn away from her gaze. I did not know what to say.

"If you had some speech prepared, you can save it. I have known about that affair since it started. I thought you were going to say that your little tramp Deanna was pregnant or something along those lines . . . maybe tell me that you were in love with her and were leaving me."

She waved off the conversation with a flip of her wrist as she poured herself a glass of water and let out a deep sigh. I felt out of place, wondering how she knew Deanna's name. She studied her glass and proceeded to concentrate on the flow of traffic outside of her window.

"I bet you are wondering how and what I know about your little hot tamale. Let's see . . . Deanna Quiones . . . age twenty-nine . . . born September 2nd . . . lives

at 7823 Candlewood Estates Drive . . .
roommates Laurie and Kendra . . . works at
Stables . . . born in Puerto Rico . . . has five
children, all wards of the State . . . ten prior
arrests including Possession of Drug
Paraphernalia and Prostitution. But I am sure
your penis was so enamored that you never
stopped to ask questions."

She spouted off Deanna's profile with
no emotion . . . she was just stating facts. I
wondered why she had known about it all
along and had never said anything. She kept
her steady gaze out of the window and
continued talking.

"I found out about her the day after
you met her because you left your cell phone
on the bed when you went to take a shower.
Her name and number popped up with a text
message saying how sexy you were and how
she couldn't wait to see you again."

I literally felt the color drain from my face. I sat in my chair, numb and quiet. Everything that I had thought about Deanna was a lie, but I was not surprised. My intuition told me that she had many secrets. I was too busy cheating that I did not think too far into the act.

"Claudia, I'm sorry . . . I didn't mean to . . ." I was not able to finish my sentence when Claudia looked at me with pure hatred in her eyes. I could not speak for fear that she would slap me from across the table.

"You are sorry, Terry. And I am sorry, too. I am sorry that I did not have the strength to stop you, to let you know that I knew what was going on from the very beginning. But guess what? I am stronger than I have EVER been in my life."

Her eyes burned with fire as she commanded the tears not to fall. The tension in her face spoke volumes, and she fought with every ounce of her being to maintain control.

"I knew about all of your little secret meetings and get-away sessions with her. I kept holding out faith that it was just a phase you were going through, and that you would remember you had a wife that loved you at home.

"But after waiting and waiting on you, I got tired. So I started following you. I knew who she was, I knew all about her, but I had never seen her until last night. I saw you go into her house."

I was starting to feel sick. I remembered how Deanna had greeted me at the door. I was looking through Claudia's eyes and imagined how she felt when she saw us. I resigned in my heart that I did not stand a chance of forgiveness.

"What kind of woman answers the door wearing lingerie? I saw her all over you at the front door, kissing you like a mad woman, jumping all over your body like you BELONGED to her. Do you belong to her, Terry?"

Claudia thought for a moment, then held her hand up, indicating to me that I was not allowed to talk. She drank the rest of her water down in one smooth stream. She sat her glass down quietly and dabbed the sides of her mouth with a handkerchief.

"I woke up this morning ready to die, Terry. I spent the day with a total stranger just to keep from killing myself. Do you know what that feels like? Pretty pathetic, let me tell you!" As she laughed at herself, I felt an unneeded jealousy rise up in me.

"So that's what you were doing today, Claudia? I was trying to spend time with you and you were out having sex with some stranger to pay me back?!" Although I had no room to judge, the thought of someone touching her body made me want to kill. She started to laugh at me.

"Oh Terry, grow up! Regardless of your behavior I have learned not to repay evil for evil. But let me tell you something . . . It's not your concern who I was with or what I was doing. I am not you." She spat the words as if I repulsed her. I had never experienced anyone treating me like I was a nobody, especially not Claudia.

Her eyes finally looked toward me, and she stared at me as if I was the most wretched sight. I knew that I had made a mistake, but I expected that I would just tell her the affair was over, and she would go back to being my wife.

"You know . . . instead of killing myself, I am deciding to love myself. You don't have to want me, 'cause I want me. You don't have to cherish me, 'cause I cherish me. I don't want the house, the jewelry, the clothes or anything that you have purchased for me. I thought I deserved those things because I was your wife . . . because I had been faithful to you and you loved me.

"But I see that you gave the same gifts of 'love' to your whore. So I don't want any of it. Give it to her."

Being the lady that she was, she stood up and politely pushed her chair back up to the table. She walked out of the restaurant with her head up, leaving me there like I was an orphan. I was NOT going to let things end like that.

I found the waiter and left my credit card in his hand. I made a bee-line to the door, hoping to catch her. I saw her waiting for the valet, and I reached out to grab her arm.

"Don't . . . ever . . . touch . . . me . . . again!" Her words came out like a slow hiss as she talked through clenched teeth. I could feel her body shaking, as if she was about to erupt in anger. I was not the type to beg her to stay, but I did not know if I would ever see her again if I let her walk away.

"Claudia, I have had enough of this foolishness. Are you just going to walk out on me like that?" I held my face close to hers and searched her expression to see if there was a modicum of feeling toward me. She tightly shut her eyes and tried to breathe deep, measured breaths.

In all of my life, I had never begged anyone for anything. I am sure I was a pitiful sight, begging her as if I was desperate. I was growing frustrated.

As the valet returned with her car, she released herself from my grip. "Meet me over at Sutter's Bridge. I will give you five minutes to talk."

She held up her hand to signify the importance of 'five' as she entered her car and drove away.

Claudia had never talked to me in such a way . . . so direct and demanding. I had always known her to be very passive and even. This woman who was speaking up and giving orders was not the wife I had a year ago . . .

I guess I had never really taken the time to get to know who she was. When we were younger, she strived to make life all about me. I hardly heard her speak about herself. She waited on me hand and foot, and gave me everything that I needed.

As I was thinking of how we used to be, I realized when things started to change. About five years ago, she was no longer content just being my wife. She started getting more serious about her business. She spent more time thinking about her own future.

She started to buy her own properties and spending more time at work. She even bought her own car. She didn't need me as much as she used to.

At that point in my thought process, instead of feeling ashamed for what I had done, I felt justified. In all of my life, my mother did not have outside jobs. She stayed home . . . she had children. She served her husband. What did Claudia do for me but share space in a house? We did not even have sex.

Deanna's words burned in my mind, that if I had not had an affair with her, that I would have had an affair with someone else. Claudia had stopped being my wife, and I needed a woman who needed me.

I jumped in my car, speedily driving to Sutter's Bridge. I told myself that I was going to give Claudia a piece of my mind, because I had every right to demand her to be what I needed her to be. How dare she talk to me about another woman when she stopped giving me what I needed?

As I drove, I felt a fire burn in my chest. I felt as if I was in a cartoon . . . where I had an angel on one shoulder and a demon on the other. The angel was telling me to apologize and do what I needed to do to make things right. The demon was telling me that Claudia failed me.

I blocked out the wise counsel and focused more on my pride. Claudia was to blame. She pushed me into the arms of Deanna, and I was prepared to tell her that if she wanted to keep me, she better start acting like a wife.

As I reached Sutter's Bridge, I saw her sitting on a large rock. Her loose hair blew in the wind, and her head was hung as if she had been praying. I almost lost my resolve when I noticed how pitiful she looked. But as a man, I could not show weakness. I walked up to where she was sitting, and started unleashing the most disrespectful tirade I had ever spoken to anyone.

"What is wrong with you, Claudia? You walked out of the restaurant, embarrassing me like some street person, making a scene. I wanted to tell you at dinner tonight that I am done with Deanna. I want to be with you, or are you too stupid to see that?" I watched as she slowly lifted her head in disbelief. She looked at me as if I had two heads, and then turned to look away.

"You know what, Terry? You're the one who was sleeping with a woman you knew nothing about. So what does that make you? If I were you, I would think twice before calling someone stupid." She looked as if she was talking to someone in the distance, making a point not to look at me. I was growing frustrated with her nonchalance, and I wanted a reaction.

"I am tired of this foolishness. You are not going to command me and give me orders. I am still the man in this relationship.

Maybe if you acted more like a wife, all of this would have never happened."

I saw a wild look come into Claudia's eyes, as she rose up from her sitting position, looking as if she was about to do damage.

"You don't think about anyone but yourself. What about your vows? What about our commitment, for better or for worse?" She screamed at the top of her lungs, walking toward me with her fists clenched.

"More like a wife, you say? More like a wife or more like a whore?" She was standing inches away from my face yelling, her hot breath warming my chin. I wanted to back down, but my pride would not allow me to flinch. I stood my ground. If she wanted to be mad, I could be mad right along with her.

"Okay! So now the real Claudia comes out . . . the little ghetto girl I rescued from the 'hood. Yes, I said it, Claudia. A WIFE. You know what it means? That is someone who spends time with me . . . someone who makes me more important than her job. Somebody that gives me some!"

She slapped me so hard that I felt the side of my face burning. Just as I was adjusting to the feel of her palm against my face, another slap came. Then her fists, pummeling my chest. She was hitting me with every ounce of strength that she had.

"You want me to be a ghetto girl, I will give you a ghetto girl! Don't make this my fault, Terry!" She screamed at me before she dug her index finger into my chest. "You remember that you didn't save me from the 'hood. I was Valedictorian at our college. Your money could not buy my intellect, you pompous bastard! I didn't have the privilege of having parents who could pay my way through school.   I   would   have   been something with or without you!"

In all of our years together, I had never seen her fighting mad. I did not like to be on the receiving end, but I had to take it. I knew that I deserved it.

"Have you forgotten that I have been there for you ALWAYS, Terry? I stayed in that house with you, putting my desires on hold while you told me to wait to have kids. I waited and waited until I could not produce a child for you. I did everything how and when you wanted and this is my reward? Did you ever realize that I got a job because I loved you enough to try and establish myself so that I could give back to you instead of always taking from you?"

I did not dare tell her to lower her voice. I kept my stone stance, anticipating the next blow that was sure to come from her.

"Well if it makes you feel better, I am sorry I worked. I am sorry I couldn't be a whore who only used you for your money. As a matter of fact, I am sorry I loved you! I guess I should have just had sex with you and pretended to like it."

I didn't want to feel anymore guilt. As immature as it seems, I wanted her to feel some responsibility in my infidelity. Maybe if she felt somewhat akin to my actions, she would be more apt to forgive me.

"Well at least she wanted me! At least she acted like I meant something. When was the last time you kissed me? When was the last time we made love?"

It was at that point that she terrified me. She sat back down on the rock and started laughing uncontrollably. She quickly removed her wedding ring and placed it on the rock. I watched as she stood up and walked away for what I believed was the last time.

"I will never EVER allow you to touch me, Terry. You replaced me." She took her cell phone and threw it against the rock she was sitting on. She threw the phone with the force of an F-5 tornado. I watched as the phone shattered in little pieces.

"Don't try to find me. I'm done." She calmly walked to her car and drove away without looking back.

I made no motion to try and stop her. I walked to the rock that she had broken her phone on, and I picked up the pieces that I could find, just needing to hold on to a piece of her.

I guess I should have been grateful that it was not my body bruised and broken against the rock. She had every right to blow my brains out.

I remembered how infuriated I felt when I thought that she had spent the day with another man . . . thinking about another man touching her. I could only imagine how she must have felt knowing that I had committed a sin against her and myself.

I felt as if all sound had been sucked out of the atmosphere, as all that I could hear was my own breath. I felt the tears before I could acknowledge them. I felt such a sad emptiness in my spirit. My sanity was regained when I realized that she was not coming back. Was I so full of myself that I didn't think she would leave me, or did I think so low of her that she would just accept my flaws and stay anyway?

I felt myself fall to the grassy earth, digging my knees deep into its softness. I felt the weight of the world fall on my back and I bent to the pressure. My head became flooded with reminders . . . my actions played in my mind like a movie.

I used to be a good man. It hurt that I could not say that anymore. I wondered how I could continue in that affair with no conscience . . . no regard. It was as if I lived under the influence during that time. Was I so full of myself that I believed I would never get caught? I spread my arms and tilted my head to the sky.

"God, forgive me . . . FORGIVE MEEEEEEEEEEE!!!!"

I felt as if the Earth had moved as I yelled in the silence. When I had raised my voice to its limit, all that was left was loneliness. I was outside in the darkness, and although God was there, my wife wasn't.

The only option that I had left was to get my life right with God. Everything that I had done I knew was wrong. My marriage may have been over, but I could not lose my soul.

I rose from my knees and wiped the grass stains from my slacks. It took so much effort to walk to my car. I did not want to think about what life would be like when I returned home.

By having Claudia and Deanna, I had my dream wife and my dream lover. Where I went wrong was not making Claudia both of those. I wanted to have my cake, and eat it too . . . but in the end the cake had become infested with maggots and made me sick to my stomach.

I started my car and proceeded to make the long journey to my empty house. As I turned on my car radio, a deep, male voice caught my attention.

"My wife and I have been married for forty years, and we still have a wonderful relationship. She knows that she can trust me and I trust her. If she ever heard anything questionable about me, I know without a shadow of a doubt that she would stand up for me and my good name . . . not just because she's my wife, but because she knows my character."

I felt myself wanting to turn the station, thinking to myself "Good for you" . . . upset that someone else could have the perfect relationship. However, no matter how much his perfection bothered me, I could not turn the station.

"Someone very close to me told me at the beginning of my marriage that I could never be faithful to my wife until I was faithful to God . . . I could never fully submit to my marriage until I was willing to submit to God. When I love and honor Him, I am commanded to love my wife, and that she respect me. As long as you keep God first, your marriage will always prosper."

"Haha, God . . . I hear you!" I let the message sink inside of my pores. During my affair, I went to church every Sunday and I never stopped serving in the Church. But I can honestly say that I had NO relationship with God. I didn't pray, I didn't seek His guidance. I only went through the motions.

I reached the house and my loneliness grew. I looked at the large house that I lived in and realized that I would be living in it all by myself.

As I got inside, I looked at my priceless paintings on the walls and all of the expensive decorations and furniture that comprised the house. I then realized why Claudia said that I could have it all. All of the money in all of the world could not make up for having someone to love. I had love, and I treated her like a possession.

I instantly hated the house and everything in it. All that I wanted was Claudia. I sat on the couch, staring into the darkness. I pulled out my cell phone and started to dial Claudia's number. Then I remembered her phone was still near Sutter's Bridge, broken into a million pieces.

I stood up and walked to the kitchen. I found Claudia's contact book in a drawer next to the refrigerator. I scanned through the numbers until I found the one that I was searching for.

I nervously dialed the number, expecting her not to talk to me. I had not been particularly nice to her over the years, but I could not think of anywhere else that she would be. As she answered the phone, I felt my stomach drop.

"Hi . . . Hello . . . ahem . . . Good Evening, Mrs. Johnson. I apologize for calling you at this hour, but this is Terry, your son-in-law. I was wondering if perhaps my wife was at your house?" I did not know what I expected her to say as I had not spoken to her in years.

"Hi, Terry. No, Honey . . . she is not here. Is she s'posed to be here?" Her tone was calm, but underneath I could tell that she was curious. I did not want to divulge too much information . . . I would rather Claudia be the one to tell her what was going on.

"I am sure she is fine. Would you mind asking her to please give me a call if she comes by? I would truly appreciate it."

"Sure, Honey . . . I sure will. You have a good night."

I hung up the phone silently. I had no way of contacting Claudia now. My only option was to wait. I turned on the television and the 11 o'clock news was just coming on. I closed my eyes and laid back, letting the sound of the television drown out any thoughts that I had.

I felt my phone vibrate on my hip and I hurriedly checked it to see if it was a message from Claudia. Instead, it was a message from Deanna.

Papi, your wife came by here today. She said that it's over between you guys. Come over! I need my fix.

Deanna's request to come over would usually excite me. After the events of the day, the message sickened me. I instantly erased the message and started to pray again. Giving up on Deanna was going to be a lot harder than I thought.

I decided to call the only person besides God that could help me. I dialed the number, but became afraid when he answered.

"Hey Terry, what can I do for you, Son?"

"Pastor, Good Evening. I am sorry to call you so late, but I really need to talk." I poured out my heart and told him the entire story, from beginning to end. When I was finished, I realized how bad it sounded.

"I don't know what to do, Pastor. I know that I messed up. I don't know how to fix this."

"Well, Terry . . . confessing your faults was the first step. You know there are many men throughout history who have fallen. Think about David, who wrote the Book of Psalms . . . the Bible says that he was a man after God's own heart, and he committed adultery with Bathsheba. Now I am not saying that there will not be consequences for your actions, but God forgives."

I took the words to heart, feeling that there would be redemption for me. I did not feel so hopeless.

"I have counseled hundreds of couples over the years, and one thing that I want you to be aware of . . . if she decides to take you back, you will have to exercise patience. During the time of rebuilding, you may say or do something that will remind her of the affair, or her feelings of inadequacy. It is your responsibility to comfort her, and to let her know that she is number one in your heart."

He then prayed with me . . . a prayer to renew our minds and hearts toward one another. He also prayed a prayer of peace, knowing that both of our hearts needed the peace of God to overcome the next phase in our marriage.

As we hung up the phone, I felt somewhat comforted. I felt a spark of hope that all was not lost. I felt forgiven and that my mind was on the right track again. I closed my eyes and said a prayer, asking God to allow Claudia to come back home.

payback

I could not believe the nerve of that man!   I was hurt-sad-furious-broken-dead-sick and I wanted to do something . . . I just didn't know what that 'something' was.

"Why did you do this to me God? How could You let him do this to me? I have been faithful! I served you! I did what a wife should do! You didn't save me!"

I yelled and spoke to God like never before. On one hand, I believed that God had given me strength to deal with Terry's infidelity.   I was raised to believe that marriage vows were followed to the letter. I stayed by my man no matter what.

I trusted God to bring Terry through his little phase and show him what he was doing was not just fundamentally wrong, but it was also spiritually wrong.

On the other hand, I was not prepared for the response that Terry gave me.   He actually felt justified sleeping with that her. I guess I had expected him to come back on bended-knee, begging and crying his heart out. It seemed like he spent more time blaming me than accepting responsibility.

How he could blame his actions on my job was beyond me. He didn't care about my feelings . . . all he cared about was himself. That's when I knew our marriage was over. No matter how long I waited, he was going to do what he wanted to do.

I knew that God was not to blame for Terry's actions, but I did not have anyone else to talk to. I kept feeling that rage consume me whenever I recalled the words that he said to me.

I tried to drive but my eyes became blurry with tears as I visualized Deanna. In my mind's eye, I kept seeing her beautiful shape and how she oozed sexuality. When

Terry looked at me, he would always compare me to her. I could not compete.

I stopped driving when my tears were too heavy to see through. I laid my head on the steering wheel and allowed them to fall with no interruption. My steering wheel and my lap were soaked by the time I lifted my head.   All of my sadness then became replaced with anger.

I wanted to hurt Terry . . . matter of fact, I wanted to kill him. I kept telling myself that I had been wronged, and that I could not allow him to get away with what he did to me.   I drove in silence, only my thoughts to keep me company.

At first, I envisioned staring at him from the barrel of a .357 Magnum. I would hold it to his head and watch him, weak and crying, beg me for mercy.

Then I imagined putting my hands around his neck, watching him slowly run out of air. My mind traveled back to how it would feel to shoot him. I didn't want to kill him. Maybe just shoot him in a place that wouldn't allow him to ever cheat on me or any other woman ever again.

Before I realized it, I ended up at my parent's house. I knew that my mother would have a lot of crazy things to say to me, but I did not care. The fact was that I did not have anywhere else that I could go.

As I looked up at their front porch, I figured that Terry had called my mother because she was sitting on her porch in her robe, smoking a cigarette, looking as if she was waiting to curse someone out. I instantly felt bad and for the second time that day, I wanted to keep driving.

I parked my car and started the long walk to the porch. I was barefoot, and I concentrated on a feeling I had not felt in years. I felt the soft grass between my toes, and the concrete touching the soles of my feet, just as I had when I was a child. A slight breeze caressed my bare shoulders and lifted the loose strands of my hair, seemingly pushing me forward.

My mother stood as I walked closer, giving me a good look over before I got too close to her. She looked like she was annoyed, but I did not stop walking.

"C, I'ma ask you ONE good time . . . what in tha world you done got yo'self into?!" I had not even gotten on the porch yet, and she was in a fighting mood.

"Yo' husband callin' me, can't nobody get ahold of you . . . You done showed up here twice in one day! You know you ain't showed yo' behind nowhere near dis house in forever."

She started pacing her porch with a frustrated gait, and I stood speechless. For some strange reason I thought that I could come to my mother and she would just listen. I could see that she did not appreciate the inconvenience.

"You come up here lookin' all crazy like you just got in a fight . . . got people worried 'bout you. What you got to say fo' yo' self? Is you off on dat end?"

She stopped her pace suddenly and looked at me, expectantly. I did not know what answer to give her.

"Mom, I just had a very bad day. This is the only other place I could go. I know I haven't been the best daughter in the world, but I thought at least you would try and be understanding. But you know what,

I'm sorry I bothered you. Next time Terry calls, just tell him I said I'll talk to him when I'm ready."

I made a motion to turn around and walk back to my car but I should have known that it wasn't going to be that easy. When Ida Mae wanted answers, she got them.

"I don't know who you think you is comin' up here commandin' people. You done already woke me up. So let's do it . . ." She sat down on her wicker chair and waited for me to come and sit beside her. I was tired, and I was in no hurry to go anywhere. Plus, I did not have a clue what my next step would be.

I took my seat next to her and stared out into the darkness for a moment. "Mom, Terry has been cheating on me for the past year." I paused for a moment, waiting for a response. When there was none, I continued.

"I finally got fed up and I kind of lost it. Right now he is trying to convince me that he's done with her, but I don't know what to believe. I am just tired."

I dropped my head in my hands and felt the heaviness come over me again. I thought to myself that if I decided to leave him, I would essentially be starting all over again, with no guarantees that the next man would be any better than the husband I am leaving.

My mother sucked her teeth and looked me straight in my face.

"Claudia, I'ma tell you somethin' you probably won't agree wit', but it is what it is. Men is men and you jus' gotta let 'em do what they do. You wastin' all yo' time and emotion tryin' to make a man be faithful, and you gonna feel like you runnin' in circles, chasin' yo' tail."

She dragged on her cigarette, sitting back contently. Her voice was calm and even, and she said her piece so nonchalantly that I realized she believed it wholeheartedly.

"You really can't be serious, Mom. There are faithful men in the world. Terry and Daddy just happen to not be one of them."

She laughed at me like I was the biggest fool that ever walked the Earth. "Oh, you think so? Show me a faithful man, and I'ma show you a man who got secrets. He probably gay if he ain't got another woman. Faithful man? Ain't no such thing!"

I felt myself getting more upset as the conversation continued. I was tired of being a weak woman, and just accepting Terry's behavior as 'normal'.

"You know, Mom . . . I remember how I used to see Daddy with different women all the time. I even remember telling you how I caught him kissing the next door neighbor. You acted like nothing that he did was wrong. Sometimes I heard you crying when you thought you were by yourself, but you never said anything to him . . . not once. He was allowed to do God knows what with God knows who, and you kept letting him come back home! And here I am, being a fool just like you!"

Before I could react, my mother was in my face, her hand raised in a position to backhand slap me.

"Look here, Lil' Girl. I don't care how much money you got, where you live or what you drive. You EVER raise your voice to me again, I'ma slap you back to the cotton fields, you hear me?"

I hung my head and murmured a low 'Yes, Ma'am', embarrassed for my outburst.

It was all misplaced anger . . . I was wanting someone to feel as bad as I felt. My mother did not take lightly to being disrespected by me.

"I'm from tha Old School, where come Hell or high-water, you stayed together. We ain't take vows to break 'em. Ya'll kids divorce over a broken nail!" She flicked her cigarette ashes over the porch railing. "When I said 'til death do me part, I meant it!"

My mother sat back down slowly, regaining her composure. I somewhat laughed on the inside, thinking that my mother had gotten soft in her older age. Twenty years prior, I would have been laid out on the sidewalk, picking up my teeth.

"But hear me when I tell ya', folks reap what they sow. Thas why yo' daddy in there dyin', goin' for dialysis treatments every three days. He sowin' right now like nobody's business!"

My mother actually laughed at the fact that my father was dying. I felt as if I were in the Twilight Zone, wondering what kind of pain she had endured to make her hate him enough to celebrate the fact that his life was coming to an end.

"You sittin' up here cryin' and actin' crazy. Trust me . . . Terry gonna reap. But don't be like me, waitin' for him to die. If he apologizin' for it, give him a chance to get right. Yo' daddy ain't never said sorry for nothin' . . ."

I looked at my mom, the woman who looked so beautiful and yet so unhappy. She looked angry and she fought back tears by lighting up another cigarette.

"Just 'cause I made my choices, don't mean you gotta make the same. If you gon' leave 'im, LEAVE. Don't waste time bein' sad about it. And pray . . . maybe if I woulda prayed more and smoked less, God woulda made him sooner."

I shook my head and hung it. I did not know what to say to my mother at that point. For the third time that day, the "Crazy" song started playing in my mind. I think my mother had truly lost it.

"Mom, you can't mean that. I know you don't mean that."

"If you think I'm lyin', you don't know nothin'. I can't wait to be free from this burden. I been tied to that man since I was thirteen. The best thing I can say I got from forty years of marriage is you."

Before I could get caught up in the emotionality of the moment, she started to laugh again. "Jesus, Claudia and Kools. That's all I got to be happy about in my life."

"Don't say that . . . please. You have the kids that you take care of. You have so many people that love you."

"Yeah, I guess you right. But all I got to call mine is Jesus, you and my cigarettes. And after yo' daddy is dead, I got that insurance money."

My mother got up and tightened her robe. I took that as my cue that our conversation was over.

"Go home, Claudia. I can't tell you nothin' that I ain't already told you. Even if Terry was a serial killa', thas still yo' house. Don't let no man put you out yo' own house."

"To be honest with you, I don't even want it. He can have it all. I just want to be happy."

She went to the front door and opened the screen, about to go back inside. She turned back and looked at me with a mixture of fatigue and sadness.

"Well jus' pray on it. God might make 'im die faster."

She did not look back toward me, neither did she bid me farewell. She just shut the door and left me standing on the porch. When I heard the click of the lock, I stood on the porch for a while.

My mind was in a confused state. I felt more depressed than I was before I saw my mother. I did not want to end up like her . . . a bitter woman who hated her husband.

I wanted to bang on the door and ask her why she stayed for so long if she hated my Daddy so much? Why just wait for a man to die?

I then understood the answer. We both fell into a routine, and we made no effort to change. We got used to being the wife who catered and accommodated that we chose to accept our role, rather than rock the boat. Our men knew that we would continue to be there, so they felt that they could do anything they wanted to.

We would always remain constant.

I was not going to be my mother. I was not going to be the old Claudia. As I walked down the steps and toward my car, I decided I was going to stop centering my life around Terry . . . now it was all about me.

I got into my car and drove far away from my mother's house. As I drove through the night with no clear destination, I thought that the only way that I would feel better about the situation was to do to Terry he had done to me.

I focused my mind on who I could have an affair with. Just about every man that I knew was a professional contact, or one of Terry's friends. I wanted to get revenge, but sleeping with one of his friends would have been too low for me. As I wracked my brain thinking of a person, a name appeared before my eyes.

Rasheed.

Rasheed is my personal trainer. He was known around the city as a ladies man, which was a nice way to say that he was a player. He has been my trainer for a little over two years, and he has flirted with me on more than one occasion.

Although I had made up my mind that he was the one, I was nervous about making that move. I drove around for a while, talking myself into and out of going forward with contacting Rasheed.

I thought about my vows, how I promised to be faithful to my husband. Then I thought about all of the nights I had slept alone over the past year . . . how I had programmed myself to not miss being loved or touched. I waited for Terry, and after all of that waiting I was still unloved and untouched.

I made up my mind to see Rasheed.

I felt around in my purse for my cell phone, only to realize that it was shattered by Sutter's Bridge. I was so upset at Terry I did not think that I would need it.

My only other option would be to just show up at his house. He did not live too far away from where I was driving. I turned my car into the direction of his house, and made my way to him.

When I reached his house, I immediately got out of the car and walked straight to his front door. I did not want to give myself the opportunity to change my mind.

I lifted my hand to knock on his front door, but stopped myself before I could knock. What if he had a woman in bed with him already? What if he told me he wasn't really attracted to me?

I started to knock anyway. I did not come that far to turn around, and it took too much nerve to make it that far. I could not let Terry get away from what he had done to me. I deserved to feel good, too.

"Who is it?!" I heard a strong male voice from behind the door, and he did not sound too happy.

"Rasheed, it's me . . . Claudia."

He opened the door quickly, looking at me with concern. He opened the door wide for me to come inside.

"Hey, Miss Claudia. Is something wrong?" I could not answer due to staring at him. He only had on his boxers and I was starting to get embarrassed.

"Ummm . . . yes . . . I'm sorry, Rasheed. I . . . uh . . . were you busy?" I felt like an idiot. What kind of woman was I to just show up at a man's house at night?

"Oh, no. I was just getting ready for bed. Unless you were coming to join me." He smiled a wolfish smile that made me want to run. But I knew what I came for, and I was not planning to leave until my mission was complete.

"May I use your restroom?" I needed an escape, and I also needed to see what I was looking like. I had just endured a rough day and night, and I did not take a moment to straighten myself before I came to Rasheed's house.

He directed me to where the bathroom was, and I stood in front of his full-length mirror straightening my hair and smoothing my dress. I stood still for a moment, truly looking at myself.

I looked at my face . . . a face that I had once considered to be pretty. I looked at my body and although I was in shape, I wasn't her. Subconsciously, I compared myself to Deanna and I felt so inadequate. How could I ensure that he could stay away from her?

I came out of the bathroom and found Rasheed, standing in the kitchen pulling out two coffee mugs. I did not say anything, I just walked over to him until I was face to face with him.

"Rasheed, I know that this is a crazy request, but can you please just hold me?" By then, I had started to cry. I was having a nervous breakdown in his kitchen, and I could not pull myself together.

He did not ask questions, he just put his arms around me. It felt so good to have male arms around me. I closed my eyes and pretended that he was Terry.

"Do you think that I'm beautiful?" I felt his lips trailing kisses down my neck to my shoulder-bone, pulling me closer to him with every kiss. In my mind I saw Terry, and I was reminded of how things used to be with us.

"I have always thought that you were beautiful, Miss Claudia. You are one of the sexiest women I have ever met. And any man who doesn't think so has to be insane." Hearing his voice snapped me out of my dreams. I was there with Rasheed and not Terry. I felt his hands moving toward the zipper on my dress.

"My husband's mistress is beautiful, Rasheed. I just wanted someone to make me feel beautiful, too." I put my hands on his jawbones and pulled his lips toward mine. I felt feelings that I had not felt in a long time. He started to undress me and my body was ready to take it all the way . . .

And then he stopped.

I stood there with my eyes closed for what felt like an eternity. When I opened them, Rasheed was just staring at me with a smile on his face. I was so emotionally raw, I did not see what could be funny.

"You know, this was a bad idea. I am sorry Rasheed, I should not have . . ."

"Miss . . .I mean, Claudia . . . I ain't never been a woman's second choice. You came over to prove a point and I was very tempted to prove it wit' you." He took my hand and led me to the kitchen counter and started the coffee maker.

"You ain't the type to get down like this. I see them types all day long at the gym. You a good girl. If I ain't have no good sense I woulda took it from you, forreal. I'm still kinda tempted to take it anyway . . ."

He playfully reached over and pulled me to him, and I unconsciously let out a laugh. I bet I looked ridiculous.

"I see women all the time who come to the gym to get back at they man, 'cause he been out cheatin' and they think they gonna get fine so he won't look at otha' women. But guess what? If it's in a man to cheat, it don't matter how fine you are. Look at Halle Berry!"

I had to agree. It was so easy for me to internalize Terry's infidelity. Somewhere in me I figured that it must be because of how I looked. All of my imperfections were magnified in my mind, because I could not reason why he would choose to cheat on me.

Rasheed sat me down at his table, poured us both a cup of coffee and he sat across from me. I was feeling stupid for coming over and bothering him and I was thinking of the easiest way to make an exit. He reached out and took my hands, and looked at me seriously.

He told me to let him know what happened, and he sat there while I told him the whole story. He did not interrupt, he just let me pour it all out for him. When I was done he finally let my hands go.

"As fine as you are, Claudia . . . you know tonight would not have gone down. But don't think for a second that you aren't beautiful or desirable."

I had to turn my head away from him. My eyes started to betray me again and the tears started falling. I felt as if he was trying to let me down easy because he didn't want me.

"So what's wrong with me, Rasheed? Am I too big? Am I too old or not sexy? Are you just being nice?" I was crying uncontrollably by then, pushing my chair back, planning to make an exit.

"Sit down, Claudia."

He spoke to me as a command, not a request. I slowly sat back down in the chair, my head heavy with shame. Being rejected by Terry was bad enough. Being rejected by Rasheed was the icing on the cake.

"From the first time I met you, you had a special place in me 'cause you reminded me of my ex-wife." I looked at him in disbelief, not knowing that he had ever been married before.

"I know it's hard to believe, but I had a wife . . . a GOOD woman. She stuck by me, and supported me in everything that I wanted to do. She helped me build my business and become successful. But I thought I couldn't be tied down . . . I thought I needed variety."

He laughed a little while he sipped his coffee, trying to make light of the conversation. I could tell that it was a sad memory for him.

"But I was an idiot, just like your husband. I thought about myself and not my wife's feelings. She turned a blind eye to most of the stuff I was doin' 'til she got to a point where she couldn't take it. She left me."

I looked at his face and saw the sadness in his eyes. He looked as if he had truly lost the love of his life.

"When she left I thought that I was free, that I had a license to sleep with any woman I wanted to. But after a while, I missed the love. I could sleep with a hundred women, but it was only my wife that actually loved me. Claudia, I know you a good woman. And your husband may not see what he has right now, but trust me . . . he will."

His words hit me in the heart. I had assumed that men could cheat with no conscience, that they just destroyed one woman after another.

"I have to apologize for coming over here like this, Rasheed. I was not thinking straight. All that was on my mind was revenge and you are the only man who came to mind. I feel so embarrassed . . ."

"Don't be embarrassed. People do strange things when they are in pain. My question is: do you still love your husband?"

Of course I love him. I have never loved any other man but Terry. My fear was that he did not love me. I had done such a good job of not voicing my fears, that I was afraid to speak them.

"It's not about me loving him, Rasheed. It's more about him loving me enough to be faithful."

"Well," Rasheed touched his chin, "I am not taking up for your husband, but people make mistakes. You said that he told you about the affair, so that must mean that he regrets it."

I was reluctant to agree with Rasheed. I did not know what to think or feel. My heart wanted to give him the benefit of the doubt, but my mind was working on an exit strategy.

I stood up and made my way to the door, with Rasheed following me all the way. All of my desire to be intimate with him had faded.

"You know, if he doesn't straighten up and see what he has, I'm here. Not just for sex, either. You are the type of woman I could definitely be with and I'm secretly hoping he don't straighten up."

He winked at me before I walked out of his door, and I was feeling rejuvenated. I felt thankful that Rasheed had willpower. I know that I would have regretted sleeping with him, but it felt good to know that someone thought I was beautiful and wanted me.

As I drove home, I no longer felt sorry for myself. I felt liberated. I was a good woman, and I deserved a faithful man. I loved Terry, but I didn't love him more than I loved my sanity. As I drove home, I vowed never to let him take my self-esteem again.

I also took time to pray and ask forgiveness for my thoughts and actions. Because of my pain, I almost committed a sin against God and myself. I was willing to do the same thing he had done to me, just so I could feel better.

Revenge was not worth my soul. I decided that I was not going to act out in anger. I was going to walk into my house and tell Terry what I deserved. It would be his choice whether or not to get with the program.

ending

I silently thanked God when I heard the garage ascending and the familiar beeps of the alarm system. I looked over at my watch and saw the time. It was a little past two o'clock in the morning.

I was still in my grass-stained trousers, barefoot and desperate. I stationed myself on the living room couch, believing that she would walk in the door at some point. I was afraid that if I left my position, she would leave and I would not see her.

She jumped when she noticed me sitting on the couch. She stopped walking for a moment, and stared at me through the darkness of the room. When she finally realized that it was me on the couch, she hurriedly kept walking.

"Claudia?" I called out her name, my voice pleading for a response. My ego had been deflated, and I was not going to act as if

I did not need my wife. All of the sudden, the Temptation's song 'Ain't Too Proud To Beg' came to my mind, and I caught myself from laughing.

"Yes, Terry . . . it's been a long day and I'm tired. If you are still trying to blame me, save it."

She held up her hand in a motion to stop my flow of conversation, and I could hear the weariness in her voice. But in addition to the weariness, I heard a new strength.

"I just need to talk to you. Please just sit down here with me so we can talk."

She flipped on the light-switch, and it was as if I was seeing her again for the first time. She was not dressed in her armor or hiding behind a wall. She was vulnerable and pretty . . . just like she had been when we first met.

"I don't trust myself to sit anywhere next to you, Terry. I just want to stand here. Whatever you have to say just say it."

"Claudia, I was out of line for blaming you for my affair. I thought that I was missing something . . . I can't say it was because you were working. I made a huge mistake and I'm sorry. I just want my marriage back."

I saw her eyes ascend upward, and she was looking as if she was annoyed by my words. I cannot imagine the thoughts that were going through her head.

"I hear you, Terry. You were missing something, but what is to say that you won't miss that 'something' in the future? How can I trust you ever again?" She kept her eyes downcast, and started to walk away from me.

"Baby." I spoke the word without thinking about its meaning or significance, and that word alone seemed to ignite Claudia's fire again.

"Don't you ever call me 'Baby'!" Her voice was raised and her fists became clenched again. "I'm not your 'Baby' anymore, Terry . . . You don't even want me."

She broke down into tears and by pure instinct, I jumped to her side to hold her. A part of me was afraid to touch her . . . scared that she might start trying to gouge my eyes out. But something told me to keep holding her, so I did not let her go.

At first, she was very resistant to my presence. After a while, she stopped fighting me and just let me hold her close to me.

"Why, Terry . . . Why?" She asked between her deep sobs and with every cry, I felt as if someone was punching me in my stomach. I could finally feel her hurt.

"I'm sorry, Claudia. If you give me another chance, I promise it will never happen again. I love you." Saying those words seemed to make her cry harder.

"Is it because of how I look? Or because I'm too old or because I couldn't give you a baby?" My arm was wet with her tears, but I did not let her go.

"No, Baby . . . No. It wasn't any of those things. I was just being stupid. I am so sorry." She pushed away from me again, making distance between us.

"All I wanted was for you to love me like I love you. I just wanted your love." I hated to hear the desperate tone of her voice, and to realize that I was the one causing her the pain that I heard.

But you know what? I can't do this right now, Terry." I reached out for her again, and she pushed me away again, walking back toward the garage. I panicked, thinking that she would leave again. I could not stand the thought.

"I'm sorry, Claudia!" I yelled it at the top of my lungs, causing her to stop in her tracks. "I was a fool to think that I needed anyone other than you. Please don't leave me."

As I was talking, I was subconsciously walking toward her. I fell to my knees where she stood, and wrapped my arms around her legs, crying uncontrollably. I half expected her to kick me in my teeth, but she just stood.

"Please, Claudia . . . please don't leave me. Please." I had no other words to say . . . all that I could do was beg.

"Do you know what makes me the most upset, Terry? The fact that I could never leave. I feel like such a weak woman .

. . knowing that I would stay with you, no matter what. I told myself over and over that I didn't need you, but in my heart I love you too much."

I was overcome by more guilt than I had ever felt. If the tables were turned, I could not guarantee that I would show the same grace or kindness. I stood up before her, wanting to pull her close to me and pretend that the whole affair was just a bad dream.

"But in loving you, I have to love myself. I deserve to be with a man who is faithful to me. I deserve to be complimented, and shown affection. I deserve to be treated like a queen. I won't accept less from you or anyone. The old Claudia is dead . . . do you understand that?"

I nodded my head in agreement. She went and sat down on the couch and I followed her and sat down next to her. I put my arm around her and surprisingly, she did not pull away.

"You know Claudia, I was sitting here thinking about a scripture, I think it's Proverbs twenty or something. It says 'He that finds a wife finds a good thing and gets favor from the Lord."

"It's Proverbs eighteen and twenty-two." She never raised her head, she just talked from her downward position.

"You're right. I was thinking about the scripture and it hit me that I had a good thing . . . you are my good thing that God gave me."

Claudia sat up straight looked ahead. "Terry, people always want to act holy when they want forgiveness. You want me to stay, but what guarantees that you won't be back with Deanna tomorrow? Where was your godliness when you were screwing her?"

I did not have any words to say to defend myself. I knew that my heart was changed, but I had no way to make her believe at that moment.

"I know that my words don't hold much weight right now, and I don't expect instant forgiveness. I have done a lot of wrongs in this marriage that I need to undo and I'm sorry. But even if it takes until our fiftieth anniversary for you to forgive me, I will wait . . . I promise you I will wait."

I gently pulled her toward my chest and laid myself back against the couch. I felt her body shake with silent sobs, as she tried to control her tears. I rubbed her back and the dam broke . . . I just allowed her to cry a river on me.

As I watched the broken tears fall from her eyes, I knew that I never wanted to make her cry, unless she was crying tears of joy. I pulled her closer to me to let her know that I was finally there for her.

I was out of words and all that I could think to do was to pray. I went back to the place that I should have started at the day that I met Deanna . . . what I should have done when I was presented with the opportunity to sleep with another woman. I vowed to be faithful to God, so that I could be faithful to my wife.

"Dear God, thank You for forgiving us of our sins. Thank You for giving us another chance, even when we mess up. God, I thank You for my beautiful wife . . . and please forgive me for not cherishing the treasure that You gave me. Forgive me for not coming to You when I needed strength to avoid temptation. Thank you for bringing my wife back home to me. Amen."

A peace fell over our house, and even if it was temporary, it felt good to have a calm atmosphere. Claudia laid across my lap and fell asleep. I wrapped my arms around her . . . partly to comfort her, and partly to make sure that she would not disappear before I woke up.

That night I had a crazy dream. In the dream, I was watching an elephant give birth. For some reason, I walked over to her and asked her if she wanted my help delivering the baby. The elephant talked back to me, telling me that if I would just rub her stomach, she would be able to push her baby out easier.

I stood under the elephant and rubbed her stomach, and I felt it rumble as the baby slid out. The baby that came out was not an elephant . . . it was a two-headed human baby.

One of the baby's faces was Claudia's, and the other was Deanna's. The elephant started talking to me, and she said, "Whichever you don't feed, will eventually die."

I looked at the two faces, and the face that was Claudia's said, "I am hungry, Terry. You won't let me die, will you?" I looked into her eyes as I heard Deanna's face talk to me.

"I'm what you want . . . gimme gimme gimme gimme . . ." Suddenly, I had an apple in my hand, and I held it in between them. Claudia's head leaned forward and took a bite of it and said, "Now you take a bite. We can share."

The head that was Deanna's grabbed the apple and ate the rest of it all in one bite, saying that she wanted it all. The elephant then wrapped its trunk around her head and removed it from the body, and when I looked at the baby, it had only one face . . . the face of Claudia.

I woke up to find that Claudia was not in my arms. I jumped up, ready to panic, searching through the house to make sure she had not left me.

I found her in the bedroom, standing in her closet, looking for something to wear. I came up behind her, and put my arms around her waist. I felt her body stiffen up, and she gently removed my arms.

"I'm not ready for that yet, Terry." I felt a little disappointed, but I just apologized and started to retreat out of the bedroom.

"Terry?" As she called my name, I felt a small hope inside and turned around to give her my attention. I started to remember that the healing process may take a while, and that I had to be patient with her, just like Pastor said.

"I have something that I need to tell you about yesterday." I braced myself for what was coming, thinking that she was going to tell me that she had slept with someone else. I looked at her, expectantly . . . waiting for the bomb to drop.

"I told you that I spent the day with a stranger to keep myself from wanting to die. But the truth is, I was with two strangers . . . A girl named Paris and her son, Jesse. I ended up giving her one of my houses, the one on Cypress."

Claudia went on to tell me the events of the day before . . . how she had met Paris and Jesse and her feelings toward them. I did not want to say anything to upset the balance of our relationship at that point. I was worried for Claudia, trusting complete strangers like that, but the look on her face showed that she felt strongly about what she had done. I took a deep breath before responding.

"Claudia, I don't want you to get hurt, but I know that you are an intelligent woman and you would not do this if you weren't sure. So I support your decision."

It was then that she walked up to me and hugged me. I realized that I should have given her support in all of her decisions from the beginning. Almost losing her opened my eyes about a lot of things concerning her, and I continue to pray that God gives me wisdom on how to uplift and honor her. When she whispered 'Thank You' into my chest, I realized that kindness and love would be my only way to win her back.

"I told Paris yesterday that I would take her and Jesse to get groceries today, and I did not want to leave them in that house with no food. I should be back after a while."

As she made a move to walk away, I grabbed her hand softly and spoke to her in a timid voice, which was unusual for me.

"Would you mind if I came with you? I would love to meet them."

I saw the thing that had alluded me for a very long time . . . her smile. I could not remember the last time I had seen her smile or spent a Saturday with her, and I hoped that we could look forward to many more days together . . . just the two of us.

"Sure, Terry . . . I would love that." I walked up until we were inches apart, and asked her gently and sweetly if I could just hold her . . .

And she said yes.

I had my wife . . . my 'good thing', and I was determined not to let her go ever again.